MIXED
& SHAKEN
Essential Cocktails

WHITE STAR PUBLISHERS

MIXED
& SHAKEN
Essential Cocktails

Gianfranco Di Niso - Davide Manzoni

Photographs by Fabio Petroni

CONTENTS

INTRODUCTION

Mixed & Shaken was born with the aim of proposing a comprehensive book to anyone interested in deepening their knowledge of the fascinating world of blended drinks. This practical and extremely clear manual is suitable for professional or aspiring bartenders, but also for people who are simply eager to create the numerous cocktails presented here in their own homes.

The book includes 260 drinks that are divided into 5 chapters: *Anytime Cocktails, Happy Hour Cocktails, After Dinner Cocktails, Cool Drinks,* and *Hot Drinks & Coffee,* in which evergreen cocktails, like the Martini Cocktail, the well-known Cuba Libre, and the Stinger, alternate with drinks that have established themselves as new classics, among which are the Caipiroska, the Cosmopolitan, the refined Apple Martini, and many wine-based drinks.

Easy-to-read and comprehensive instructions dedicated to each of the cocktails are subdivided into the following sections: Method, Ingredients (in American ounces for freestyle professional bartenders and in centiliters for everyone else), Preparation, and Suggested Use.

Two elements that are often ignored by the literature on blended drinks enrich the pages: the alcohol and calorie contents. This choice is certainly consistent with the professionality of bartenders who are increasingly aware of the importance of proposing cocktails with an adequate alcohol content and of educating drink lovers to drink healthy and responsibly in accordance with the Rules of the Road.

Over the last few years, fellow bartenders devoted themselves, with excellent results, to the art of the "home made," preparations that can replace syrups, liqueurs, bitters, etc., and that have personalized and enhanced the quality of many bars. However, the philosophy that has characterized my books for a decade is to democratize the knowledge of blended drinks so that it can be approached by nonprofessionals as well. For this reason, *Mixed & Shaken* almost exclusively includes affordable but also high-quality ingredients and preparations. This, of course, in no way excludes the fine practice of the "home made," which I use and which has always fascinated me.

In line with my desire to make this book accessible to all people who love blended drinks, I took the liberty of making changes in some recipes where the ingredients would have been hard to find for nonprofessionals.

Moreover, ten bartenders collaborated with me in *Mixed & Shaken*. Some of them are old friends, some are more recent acquaintances, but all of them are professionals who generously contributed to bringing prestige to this book, thanks to the recipes they created.

Let's now move to a little bit of history. The origins of the word "cocktail" are still uncertain but are linked to several legends. Below are the most accredited ones.

The first one mentions a bartender who set sail on the Mississippi River. In order to help relieve the boredom that sometimes affected the passengers, he loved trying to create excellent and brightly colored drinks that he then served to his fellow travelers in funny carafes shaped like cockerels.

According to other sources, the term "cocktail" traces its origins back to the informal English language of the 18th century, when this word was used to refer to half-blood horses, thus emphasizing the combination of different elements, just as it happens in the preparation of a drink.

Among the most original theories are the stories about a Mexican bartender from Veracruz, who used to create drinks by combining liqueurs, fruit, and fruit juices and served them garnished with a spectacular cock's tail. A reference to cockfights can be found in the legend about the marriage between a girl from Baltimore named Bessie and her sweetheart. Their union was persistently impeded by her father, a tavern owner. When the favorite rooster of the family stable disappeared, he publicly promised that in exchange for its retrieval, he would agree to the unwanted marriage. Just as in a fairy tale, the rooster was soon retrieved, and the girl could fulfill her love dream. To celebrate, Bessie combined different liqueurs, thus creating a bright-colored drink that she called "cocktail," in honor of the precious bird.

The first fully fledged guide to blended drinks was published in 1862, when Jerry Thomas, who is considered the first master bartender in history, designed the *Bartender's Guide*, a vade mecum containing several recipes that would be constantly updated with the most successful drinks. It was only at the end of the 19th century that cocktails began to be successful among the general public. As a result, bartenders were encouraged to create new cocktails, to experiment with innovative blends, and to publish increasingly comprehensive manuals. Among the most famous ones is the *Cocktail Boothby's American Bartender*. As early as 1891, this manual already included more than 350 recipes, which, for the first time, were enriched with several tricks of the trade that best explained their preparation.

The choice of a spirit as an ingredient in a drink was not only the result of the creativity or the personal taste of a bartender. External events often affected this choice, as in 1893, when in Europe, the uncontrollable proliferation of the phylloxera, an insect imported from America, destroyed almost all the grapevines. This caused the production of spirits obtained from grapes to plummet. Bartenders were forced to find a solution. Thus, they modified drinks based on cognac or brandy, replacing them with gin, vodka, or calvados, thereby creating new and successful drinks. At the beginning of the 20th century, the scourge of alcoholism was devastating Europe, where the abuse of absinthe was particularly widespread. In order to deal with the emergency, in 1915 half of Europe banned the "Fée Verte" ("Green Fairy") and all those alcoholic beverages that included this herbaceous plant among their ingredients. Overseas in 1919, in the United States after the First World War, the era of Prohibition started under the pressure of political and religious groups. During this period, the production, trade, and consumption of alcoholic beverages were banned for 15 years. One of the consequences was the development of gangsterism. This was a period of crime, and among its protagonists was Al Capone, who was able to amass a great fortune in a very short time by producing and smuggling alcohol. In 1933, after Prohibition ended, the liberal era of the tiki bars started. These were bars characterized by an exotic decor, in which elaborate cocktails were mainly served. Among the main contributors to tiki bars was the actor Donn Beach, who opened the Don the Beachcomber bar in Hollywood, which went down in history for its rum-based cocktails served in extravagant glasses. If we think of the American Dream with respect to bartenders, the Californian Victor J.

Bergeron deserves to be mentioned. He was a skilled entrepreneur who, during the '40s, managed to open a tiki bar chain that became such a great and long-lasting success that it survived the tragedy of the Second World War, prolonging its activity in the following decades. In the '70s, bartenders created some of the most successful long drinks, like the Gin and Tonic or the Vodka Tonic, which are still appreciated today.

In the mid-1980s, the concept of bartending was revolutionized by the techniques of "Freestyle" and "Flair" bartending. The latter became a real fashion following the release of *Cocktail*, a 1988 movie directed by Roger Donaldson that starred a very young Tom Cruise as an acrobatic bartender. The 1980s also saw the birth of a new trend that pushed movie and music stars to invest in often-themed cocktail bars and restaurants, further attracting the public interest in the world of drinks. Burt Reynolds was the first to realize the potential of this business, followed in 1991 by Sylvester Stallone, Bruce Willis, and Arnold Schwarzenegger, who inaugurated the well-known Planet Hollywood restaurant chain in New York.

I will conclude by staying on the subject of cinema. Since I have always been a Seventh Art lover and a regular visitor to cinemas, I decided to give readers 40 short inserts that will reveal how many cocktails became protagonists on the big screen. Do you know the favorite cocktail of James Bond, the most famous secret agent in the history of cinema? And do you know the name of the drink that Humphrey Bogart and Ingrid Bergman, in love with each other, sip in *Casablanca*? You will find the answers and much more by leafing through *Mixed & Shaken*, while preparing a cocktail.

Gianfranco Di Niso

NOTE

For every cocktail recipe featured in the book, the alcohol content and the calorie content are given. The provided numerical value for the alcohol content is to be understood as an estimate, and the one for the calorie content as approximate. Even though these values are calculated with precise mathematical formulas, they might change depending on the kind and brand of the spirits used. Therefore, it has been decided to provide estimated and approximate values in order to leave freedom of choice regarding the products to be used in the creation of every cocktail.

INSTRUMENTS

THE GRADUATED CYLINDER (JIGGER)

The graduated cylinder is an indispensable tool that will allow readers to consistently prepare cocktails the same way, respecting the measurements indicated in the recipes. Graduated cylinders can be plastic or glass, and you can find them in pharmacies, chemical laboratories, plastic-producing factories, hardware stores, and other stores that sell rubber products.

THE CONTINENTAL SHAKER (ALSO CALLED TRADITIONAL SHAKER)

The symbolic bartending tool, the shaker is essential to blend the best ingredients. Shakers are divided into 3 parts: a lower part (steel, glass, or plastic) that serves as a container for ice and various ingredients; an upper part that consists of a perforated cap that acts as a filter, keeping out everything that should not end up in the glass (ice, fruit, spices, etc.); and a second upper part that consists of the cap (or lid), which crucially keeps the ingredients in place during the act of shaking. The cap can also be used as a dispenser for liquid ingredients.The three parts of the shaker must be perfectly joined together. Cocktails can be poured by simply opening the lid.

THE FRUIT KNIFE

It is advisable to have a variety of knives, in different sizes and shapes, with both smooth and serrated blades, in order to cut or engrave different fruits and vegetables.

THE MIXING GLASS

This is used in the preparation of drinks that do not need to be shaken. It can, however, be replaced with a Boston shaker, which is used by professional bartenders around the world. It is nevertheless required to make certain famous drinks, like the Martini and the Manhattan.

THE LEMON SQUEEZER

This juicing tool is used in the kitchen for squeezing citrus fruits to extract the juice. The juice is obtained by cutting fruits into two parts and squeezing them against the top cone, using a rotary motion to get the most juice possible.

THE MILK JUG

The milk jug, made of steel and equipped with a handle and different sized spouts, is used to prepare all hot drinks, thus replacing glass, which can not stand up to the heat.

THE PESTLE

Made of plastic, wood, or marble, the pestle is used in the preparation of "crushed" cocktails, such as in the Caipirinha family. Generally, it is used to crush mint with sugar and citrus.

THE STRAINER

When preparing cocktails that do not require the use of a shaker, this steel tool is essential to prevent ice from being poured into the glass.

CALIPER

It can be used either to handle ice or to place decorations on the rim of the glass or into the drink, thus avoiding the use of hands.

WHISK

This tool is used to effectively mix the ingredients of a cocktail.

THE BLENDER

The blender or food processor is a tool used for blending two or more liquid or solid ingredients. It has different speeds and may be made of plastic or steel. Sometimes the top jar is made of glass. It is an indispensable tool for preparing cocktails of various families: the Caribbean Colada, the Brazilian Batida, American frozen drinks, and sherbets made with ice cream.

ANYTIME COCKTAILS

This category is also known by the name of "popular drinks," and it includes recently created cocktails that have been consistently appreciated by the general public. The peculiarity of the Anytime cocktails is that they can be enjoyed from the early afternoon until late at night.

Especially recommended as refreshments in hot weather, these drinks are ideal to accompany a pleasant night in a bar, and they are even better if sipped between dances at a nightclub. These drinks, more than any others, can enhance the talent of bartenders, who can freely show their flair for best combining flavors, scents, shapes, and colors by using liqueurs, spirits, fruit juices, and syrups of any kind. Within this category of drinks, a fundamental role is played by their spectacular presentation, in which original glasses and fresh fruit compositions, sometimes very elaborate or artistic, become protagonists. The family of the Brazilian Batidas, which has introduced cachaça to the whole world, plays an important role among Anytime drinks. The Batidas are rich in exotic flavors, and the generous presence of tropical fruit is also able to attenuate the edgy taste of the Brazilian spirit.

Among the ancestors of the Anytime cocktails family is the Sex on the Beach, born in the '80s. This drink achieved immediate success among young people, attracted not only by its widely appreciated fruity taste, but also by a name that evokes romantic summer evenings on the seashore. It is impossible not to mention the Long Island Iced Tea, a well-known long drink that recalls iced tea both in its color and its taste. This drink is a rare exception among the Anytime cocktails because its alcohol content is highe, and therefore it must be drunk in moderation.

Among the not-to-miss drinks of this category are the Gin and Tonic, the Mai Tai, and the Cuba Libre, which all occupy a prominent position because they represent all that a good Anytime drink should be: an excellent long drink able to liven up afternoons and evenings with friends.

ANYTIME COCKTAILS

ALABAMA SLAMMER

Shake and Strain method

INGREDIENTS

dry vodka or sloe gin ¾ oz (2.5 cl)
Amaretto Disaronno ¾ oz (2.5 cl)
Southern Comfort ¾ oz (2.5 cl)
orange juice 2 oz (6 cl)
grenadine syrup (optional) ½ oz
(1.5 cl)

PREPARATION

Measure ¾ oz (2.5 cl) of dry vodka
or sloe gin in a jigger and pour into
a shaker. Repeat with ¾ oz (2.5 cl)
of Amaretto Disaronno, ¾ oz (2.5
cl) of Southern Comfort, 2 oz (6 cl)
of orange juice and ½ oz (1.5 cl) of
grenadine syrup. Add some ice cubes
and shake vigorously for a few seconds.
Holding the ice back with a strainer,
strain the drink into a tall tumbler filled
with ice and serve, garnished with
½ an orange slice, 2 cocktail cherries,
and 2 long straws.

SUGGESTED USE

A long refreshing drink, perfect throughout
the day.

APACHE

Building method

INGREDIENTS

White Port 1 oz (3 cl)
bitter (Campari bitter
is recommended)
¾ oz (2.5 cl)
orange juice 2 oz (6 cl)
grapefruit juice 1 oz (3 cl)
grenadine syrup ½ oz (1.5 cl)

PREPARATION

Measure 1 oz (3 cl) of White Port
in a jigger and pour into a tall
tumbler filled with ice. Repeat with
¾ oz (2.5 cl) of bitter, 2 oz
(6 cl) of orange juice, 1 oz (3 cl)
of grapefruit juice and ½ oz (1.5
cl) of grenadine syrup. Stir for a few
seconds with a long-handled spoon
and serve garnished with 2 long
straws, 1 wedge of orange, 1 wedge
of lemon, 2 cocktail cherries, and
1 sprig of mint.

SUGGESTED USE

An excellent aperitif to enjoy
throughout the day.

BAHAMA MAMA

Shake and Strain method

INGREDIENTS

dark rum 1 oz (3 cl)
Malibu liqueur ½ oz (1.5 cl)
pineapple juice 2 oz (6 cl)
banana cream ½ oz (1.5 cl)
orange juice 1 oz (3 cl)
grenadine syrup ½ oz (1.5 cl)

PREPARATION

Measure 1 oz (3 cl) of dark rum in
a jigger and pour in a shaker. Repeat
with ½ oz (1.5 cl) of Malibu liqueur,
½ oz (1.5 cl) of banana cream,
1 oz (3 cl) of orange juice, 2 oz (6 cl)
of pineapple juice and ½ oz (1.5 cl)
of grenadine syrup. Add some ice
cubes and shake vigorously for a few
seconds. Holding the ice back with a
strainer, strain the drink into a tall tumbler
filled with ice. Serve garnished with
½ a pineapple slice, ½ an orange slice,
3 cocktail cherries, and 2 long straws.

SUGGESTED USE

A good long drink that can be enjoyed
at any hour of the day.

BARBARA WINE

Shake and Strain method

INGREDIENTS

Müller-Thurgau wine 1½ oz
(4.5 cl)
Maraschino liqueur ½ oz (1.5 cl)
pineapple juice 3 oz (9 cl)
strawberry juice ½ oz (1.5 cl)
grenadine syrup ½ oz (1.5 cl)

PREPARATION

Measure all the ingredients in a jigger
and pour them into a shaker. Add a
few ice cubes and shake vigorously
for a few seconds. Holding the ice
back with a strainer, strain the drink into
a tall tumbler filled with ice and serve
garnished with 2 long straws, ½ a slice
of pineapple, and 2 cocktail cherries.

SUGGESTED USE

A great thirst-quenching drink enjoyable
throughout the day.

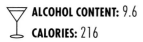
BATIDA DE COCO

Blending method

INGREDIENTS

cachaça 1½ oz (4.5 cl)
white or cane sugar 1 tbsp. (20 g)
approx.
simple syrup ¾ oz (2.5 cl)
coconut puree 1 oz (3 cl)

PREPARATION

Measure 1½ oz (4.5 cl) of cachaça
in a jigger and pour into a blender.
Repeat with ¾ oz (2.5 cl) of simple
syrup and 1 oz (3 cl) of coconut puree.
Add 1 tbsp. (20 g) approximately of
white or cane sugar, ½ a low tumbler
of crushed ice, and blend for 15–20
seconds. Pour into a tall tumbler and
serve, garnished with a few pieces of
fresh coconut and 2 long straws.

SUGGESTED USE

A tasty drink to enjoy at all hours of the day.

BITTER SWEET

Blending method

ALCOHOL CONTENT: 10.8
CALORIES: 203

INGREDIENTS

Aperol 1 oz (3 cl)
bitter (Campari bitter is
recommended) ½ oz (1.5 cl)
peach vodka 1 oz (3 cl)
peach ice cream 5¼ oz (100 g)
approx.

PREPARATION

Measure 1 oz (3 cl) of Aperol in a
jigger and pour into a blender. Repeat
with ½ oz (1.5 cl) of bitter, and 1 oz
(3 cl) of peach vodka. Add 5¼ oz
(100 g) approximately of peach ice
cream and ½ a low tumbler of crushed
ice. Blend for 15–20 seconds and pour
into a tall tumbler. Serve, garnished with
wedges of orange or fresh peach and 2
long straws.

SUGGESTED USE

A very enjoyable aperitif.

BLUE HAWAIAN COLADA

Blending method

INGREDIENTS

light rum 1 oz (3 cl)
Blue Curaçao 1 oz (3 cl)
pineapple juice 3 oz (9 cl)
coconut puree 1 oz (3 cl)

PREPARATION

Measure 1 oz (3 cl) of light rum
and 1 oz (3 cl) of Blue Curaçao
in a jigger and pour into a
blender. Repeat with 3 oz (9 cl)
of pineapple juice and 1 oz (3 cl)
of coconut puree. Add ½ a low
tumbler of crushed ice and blend for
15–20 seconds, then pour it all into
a tall tumbler. Serve, garnished with
½ a slice of pineapple, 2 cocktail
cherries, and 2 long straws.

SUGGESTED USE

A delicious drink perfect for the
afternoon and evening.

BLUE LAGOON

Shake and Strain method

INGREDIENTS

dry vodka 1½ oz (4.5 cl)
Blue Curaçao ¾ oz (2.5 cl)
lemon or lime juice 1 oz (3 cl)

PREPARATION

Measure 1½ oz (4.5 cl) of dry vodka in
a jigger and pour into a shaker. Repeat
with 1 oz (3 cl) of lemon or lime juice
and ¾ oz (2.5 cl) of Blue Curaçao.
Add some ice cubes and shake
vigorously for a few seconds. Strain
into a pre-chilled cup, holding the
ice back with the strainer, and serve,
garnished with a slice of lemon.

SUGGESTED USE

A superb digestif.

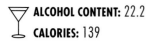

ALCOHOL CONTENT: 22.2
CALORIES: 139

BLUE MARGARITA

Shake and Strain method

INGREDIENTS

tequila 1½ oz (4.5 cl)
Blue Curaçao ¾ oz (2.5 cl)
Cointreau or triple sec ½ oz (1.5 cl)
lemon or lime juice ¾ oz (2.5 cl)
fine salt

PREPARATION

Take a sombrero glass previously chilled in the freezer and moisten half of its rim with some lemon or lime. Dip the glass into a small bowl filled with fine salt so as to coat the rim with it. Measure 1½ oz (4.5 cl) of tequila in a jigger and pour into a shaker. Repeat with ¾ oz (2.5 cl) of Blue Curaçao, ½ oz (1.5 cl) of Cointreau or triple sec, and ¾ oz (2.5 cl) of lemon or lime juice. Add ice cubes and stir for a few seconds. Strain the drink into the sombrero gass, holding the ice back with the strainer, and serve.

SUGGESTED USE

Suitable for all hours of the evening, this drink is becoming more and more fashionable as an aperitif.

CAIPIRIÑHA

Muddler method

ALCOHOL CONTENT: 18.9
CALORIES: 213

INGREDIENTS

½ lime
white or cane sugar 1 tbsp.
(20 g) approx.
cachaça 2 oz (6 cl)

PREPARATION

Place ½ a lime, cut into cubes, and 1 tbsp. (20 g) approximately of white or cane sugar in a low tumbler. Grind everything with a pestle to pulp. Fill the glass with crushed ice and pour 2 oz (6 cl) of cachaça (previously measured in a jigger). Stir for a few seconds with a long-handled spoon so as to best mix the ingredients. Serve, garnished with 2 short straws.

SUGGESTED USE

A cult drink for happy hour and perfect for after dinner as well.

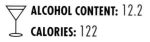

CHEROKEE

Building method

INGREDIENTS

gin 1 oz (3 cl)
bitter (Campari Bitter is
recommended) ¾ oz (2.5 cl)
orange juice 2 oz (6 cl)
grapefruit juice 1 oz (3 cl)
grenadine syrup ½ oz (1.5 cl)

PREPARATION

Measure 1 oz (3 cl) of gin in a jigger
and pour into a tall tumbler filled with
ice. Repeat with ¾ oz (2.5 cl) of bitter,
2 oz (6 cl) of orange juice, 1 oz (3 cl)
of grapefruit juice, and ½ oz (1.5 cl)
of grenadine syrup. Mix the ingredients
well with a long-handled spoon and
serve, garnished with 2 long straws,
2 cocktail cherries, a sprig of mint,
and 2 orange slices.

SUGGESTED USE

A perfect long drink for happy hour.

WHISKEY AND COLA

ALCOHOL CONTENT: 12.4
CALORIES: 156

Building method

Thelma & Louise *is a road movie by Ridley Scott that has become a feminist classic. It tells the story of two friends, Thelma (Geena Davis) and Louise (Susan Sarandon), who flee to Mexico after a murder. At the beginning of their journey, Thelma orders a Whiskey and Cola at a bar. In 1991, audiences confirmed the success of this movie, the two actresses, and this long drink.*

INGREDIENTS
whiskey (preferably American)
1½ oz (4.5 cl)
cola 4 oz (12 cl)

PREPARATION
Measure 1½ oz (4.5 cl) of whiskey in a jigger and pour into a tall tumbler filled with ice. Fill almost to the brim with 4 oz (12 cl) of cola and stir with a long-handled spoon. To serve, garnish with a lemon slice and 2 long straws.

SUGGESTED USE
Beloved by the younger crowd, this drink is suitable for any time of the day.

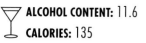

ALCOHOL CONTENT: 11.6
CALORIES: 135

CUBA LIBRE

Building method

INGREDIENTS

light or amber rum 1½ oz (4.5 cl)
lemon or lime juice ½ oz (1.5 cl)
cola 4 oz (12 cl)

PREPARATION

Measure 1½ oz (4.5 cl) of light or
amber rum in a jigger and pour into a
tall tumbler filled with ice. Repeat with
½ oz (1.5 cl) of lemon or lime juice.
Fill almost to the brim with 4 oz (12
cl) of cola and stir for a few seconds.
Serve, garnished with 2 long straws and
a slice of lime or lemon.

SUGGESTED USE

An excellent long drink appreciated all over
the world.

FROZEN DAIQUIRI

Blending method

ALCOHOL CONTENT: 12.3
CALORIES: 142

INGREDIENTS

light or amber rum 2 oz (6 cl)
lemon or lime juice 1 oz (3 cl)
simple syrup 1 oz (3 cl)

PREPARATION

Measure 2 oz (6 cl) of light or amber
rum in a jigger and pour into a blender.
Repeat with 1 oz (3 cl) of lemon or lime
juice, and 1 oz (3 cl) of simple syrup.
Add ½ tall tumbler of crushed ice and
blend for 15–20 seconds. Pour into a low
tumbler and garnish with 1 slice of lemon
and 2 short straws.

SUGGESTED USE

A great refreshing and digestive drink.

DOLCE GRECIA
(SWEET GREECE)

Shake and Strain method

INGREDIENTS

sweet Samos wine 1½ oz
(4.5 cl)
lemon or lime juice ¾ oz (2.5 cl)
simple syrup ½ oz (1.5 cl)

PREPARATION

Measure 1½ oz (4.5 cl) of sweet
Samos wine in a jigger and pour
into a shaker. Repeat with ¾ oz (2.5
cl) of lemon or lime juice and ½ oz
(1.5 cl) of simple syrup. Add a few ice
cubes and shake vigorously for a few
seconds. Holding the ice back with a
strainer, strain the drink into a cocktail
cup pre-chilled in the freezer and serve.

SUGGESTED USE

Excellent after-meal drink.

ALCOHOL CONTENT: 6.3
CALORIES: 62

ENERGY

Building method

INGREDIENTS

red vermouth 1 ½ oz (4.5 cl)
ACE juice (carrot, orange, and
lemon juice) 2 oz (6 cl)

PREPARATION

Measure 1 ½ oz (4.5 cl) of red
vermouth in a jigger and pour
into a low tumbler filled with ice.
Repeat with 2 oz (6 cl) of ACE juice
previously measured in a jigger. Stir
gently for a few seconds with a long-
handled spoon and serve, garnished
with 2 short straws and some orange,
lemon, and lime slices.

SUGGESTED USE

An excellent and energy-boosting aperitif.

ALCOHOL CONTENT: 10.8
CALORIES: 115

ERIKA
by Vincenzo Giaimo
Shake and Strain method

INGREDIENTS

gin ½ oz (1.5 cl)
freshly squeezed orange juice
½ oz (1.5 cl)
sherry 1 oz (3 cl)
vanilla liqueur 1 oz (3 cl)
ground cinnamon ¼ tsp. (1.5 g)
approx.

PREPARATION

Measure ½ oz (1.5 cl) of gin in a
jigger and pour into a shaker. Repeat
with ½ oz (1.5 cl) of freshly squeezed
orange juice, 1 oz (3 cl) of sherry,
1 oz (3 cl) of vanilla liqueur, and ¼
tsp. (1.5 g) approximately of ground
cinnamon. Add plenty of ice cubes and
shake vigorously for a few seconds.
Holding the ice back with a strainer,
strain the drink into a cocktail glass
prechilled in the freezer. Serve garnished
with a few cocktail cherries.

SUGGESTED USE

A great drink to enjoy at happy hour.

ALCOHOL CONTENT: 13.6
CALORIES: 89

ALCOHOL CONTENT: 15.8
CALORIES: 210

FRENCH KISS

Blending method

INGREDIENTS

Aperol 2 oz (6 cl)
bitter (Campari bitter
is recommended)
¾ oz (2.5 cl)
Grand Marnier
¾ oz (2.5 cl)
ACE (orange/carrot/lemon)
ice cream 5¼ oz (100 g) approx.

PREPARATION

Measure 2 oz (6 cl) of Aperol in a
jigger and pour into a blender. Repeat
with ¾ oz (2.5 cl) of Grand Marnier
and ¾ oz (2.5 cl) of bitter. Add
5¼ oz (100 g) approximately of ACE
ice cream and ½ a low tumbler of
crushed ice. Blend for 15–20 seconds
and pour into a tall tumbler. Serve,
garnished with ½ a slice of pineapple,
2 cocktail cherries, and 2 long straws.

SUGGESTED USE

A delicious aperitif.

GIN FIZZ

Shake and Strain method

ALCOHOL CONTENT: 12.6
CALORIES: 108

INGREDIENTS

gin 1½ oz (4.5 cl)
lemon or lime juice
1 oz (3 cl)
simple syrup ½ oz (1.5 cl)
soda water or sparkling
water 2 oz (6 cl)

PREPARATION

Measure 1½ oz (4.5 cl) of gin in a
jigger and pour into a shaker. Repeat
with 1 oz (3 cl) of lemon or lime juice
and ½ oz (1.5 cl) of simple syrup. Add
some ice cubes and shake vigorously
for a few seconds. Holding the ice back
with a strainer, strain the drink into a tall
tumbler filled with ice and fill with 2 oz
(6 cl) of soda water previously measured
in a jigger. Stir gently with a long-handled
spoon and serve, garnished with 2 long
straws, 2 cocktail cherries, and ½ a slice
of lemon.

SUGGESTED USE

This long drink can be enjoyed at all hours
of the day, but it is ideal during the hottest
hours. It has excellent digestive properties.

 **ALCOHOL CONTENT:** 12.3
CALORIES: 108

GIN LEMON
Building method

INGREDIENTS
gin 1½ oz (4.5 cl)
lemon soda 4 oz (12 cl)

PREPARATION
Measure 1½ oz (4.5 cl) of gin in a
jigger and pour into a tall tumbler filled
with ice. Fill almost to the brim with 4
oz (12 cl) of lemon soda and serve,
garnished with 2 long straws.

SUGGESTED USE
Magnificently refreshing, this drink is perfect
to enjoy during the hottest hours of the day.

GIN AND TONIC

Building method

FIFTY SHADES
OF GREY

Among the more or less secret passions of the mysterious Seattle billionaire Christian Grey (Jamie Dornan) are not only the bondage and sadomasochistic practices in which he involves his partners, but also gin, of which he prefers certain brands and which he drinks with tonic water and cucumber. This recipe started a trend that, since 2015, has spread to all the hottest bars of the moment.

INGREDIENTS

gin 1½ oz (4.5 cl)
tonic water 4 oz (12 cl)

PREPARATION

Measure 1½ oz (4.5 cl) of gin in a jigger and pour into a tall tumbler filled with ice. Add 4 oz (12 cl) of tonic water. Serve garnished with 2 long straws and a slice of lemon or lime.

SUGGESTED USE

This long drink is perfect for every hour of the day and excellent as an aperitif.

GRAN MARGARITA

Shake and Strain method

INGREDIENTS

dark tequila 1½ oz (4.5 cl)
Grand Marnier 1 oz (3 cl)
lemon or lime juice ¾ oz (2.5 cl)
fine salt

PREPARATION

Take a sombrero glass previously chilled in the freezer and moisten half of its rim with some lemon or lime. Dip the glass into a small bowl filled with fine salt so as to coat the damp rim with it. Measure 1½ oz (4.5 cl) of dark tequila in a jigger and pour into a shaker. Repeat with 1 oz (3 cl) of Grand Marnier and ¾ oz (2.5 cl) of lemon or lime juice. Add some ice cubes and shake vigorously for a few seconds. Strain the drink into the sombrero glass, holding the ice back with the strainer to serve.

SUGGESTED USE

A drink that can be enjoyed throughout the evening.

HARVEY WALLBANGER

Building method

ALCOHOL CONTENT: 17.8

CALORIES: 190

Harvey Wallbanger means "drunk driver" in CB radio slang. This cool and stylish cocktail is ordered for everyone in a bar during this amusing 1980 comedy starring Gene Wilder and Richard Pryor. The two friends, one blind and the other deaf, get unwillingly involved in a murder that turns their world upside down, giving rise to a series of hilarious gags.

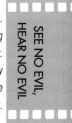

SEE NO EVIL,
HEAR NO EVIL

INGREDIENTS

dry vodka 1½ oz (4.5 cl)
orange juice 3 oz (9 cl)
Galliano liqueur ¾ oz (2.5 cl)

PREPARATION

Measure 1½ oz (4.5 cl) of dry vodka in a jigger and pour into a tall tumbler filled with ice. Repeat with 3 oz (9 cl) of orange juice and stir with a long-handled spoon. Measure ¾ oz (2.5 cl) of Galliano liqueur in a jigger and lay it on the other ingredients with the help of the spoon. Serve, garnished with 2 long straws, 2 cocktail cherries, and ½ an orange slice.

SUGGESTED USE

This long drink can pleasantly surprise you at all hours of the day.

ANYTIME COCKTAILS   37

Evita, a captivating 1996 musical film directed by Alan Parker, was
a celebration of the glorious but unfortunate life of Evita Peron,
played by a flawless Madonna. During a horse race, several extras
playing the role of the Buenos Aires elite sip the Horse's Neck, which
experienced a worldwide revival thanks to the success of Evita.

HORSE'S NECK

Building method

INGREDIENTS

cognac 1½ oz (4.5 cl)
ginger ale 4 oz (12 cl)
angostura 1 dash (2–3 drops)
(optional)

PREPARATION

Measure 1½ oz (4.5 cl) of cognac in
a jigger, pour into a tall tumbler filled
with ice, and add a dash (2–3 drops)
of angostura. Fill almost to the brim with
4 oz (12 cl) of ginger ale and serve,
garnished with ½ an orange slice and
2 long straws.

SUGGESTED USE

A good long drink suitable for all hours of
the day.

ALCOHOL CONTENT: 10.8
CALORIES: 108

HOT EXPLOSION

Blending method

INGREDIENTS

white vermouth 1¼ oz (4 cl)
banana puree or smoothie 1 oz (3 cl)
peach puree or smoothie 1 oz (3 cl)
orange juice 1 oz (3 cl)
chili powder ½ tps.

PREPARATION

Measure all the wet ingredients in a jigger
and pour into a blender together with ½
a teaspoon of chili powder and ½ a low
tumbler of crushed ice. Blend for 15–20
seconds and pour into a tall tumbler.
Serve, garnished with 2 long straws and
a dusting of chili powder.

SUGGESTED USE

A drink especially recommended for
"passionate" occasions.

ALCOHOL CONTENT: 7.3
CALORIES: 143

HUGO

Building method (sparkling version with no ice)

INGREDIENTS

elderflower syrup 1 oz (3 cl)
brut sparkling wine or
Champagne 2 oz (6 cl)
sparkling water or soda water
(ice-cold) 2 oz (6 cl)

PREPARATION

Measure 1 oz (3 cl) of elderflower
syrup in a jigger and pour into a
wine glass. Repeat with 2 oz (6 cl)
of ice-cold brut sparkling wine or
Champagne and 2 oz (6 cl) of ice-
cold soda water or sparkling water.
Stir gently for a few seconds and
serve, garnished with 1 sprig of mint
and 1 lemon wedge.

SUGGESTED USE

Mainly known as an excellent aperitif,
this drink is also enjoyable throughout the
day. In the classic version, the glass must
be filled with ice.

ALCOHOL CONTENT: 7.6
CALORIES: 146

I DUE GOLFI
(THE TWO GULFS)

by Renato Pinfildi

Shake and Strain method

INGREDIENTS

mezcal 1 oz (3 cl)
Italian dry gin 1 oz (3 cl)
Annurca apple liqueur ¼ oz (1 cl)
fresh lime juice ½ oz (1.5 cl)
fresh Sorrento lemon juice ¼ oz (1 cl)
agave honey ¾ oz (2 cl)
tabasco 1 dash (2 drops)
Hawaii black salt

PREPARATION

Take a cocktail glass previously chilled in the
freezer and moisten half of its rim with some
lemon. Dip the glass into a small bowl filled
with Hawaii black salt so as to coat the damp
rim with it. Measure 1 oz (3 cl) of mezcal in
a jigger and pour into a shaker. Repeat with
1 oz (3 cl) of gin, ¼ oz (1 cl) of Annurca
apple liqueur, ¼ oz (1 cl) of fresh Sorrento
lemon juice, and ½ oz (1.5 cl) of fresh lime
juice. Add 1 dash (2 drops) of tabasco,
¾ oz (2 cl) of agave honey, and some ice
cubes. Shake vigorously for a few seconds
then, holding the ice back with a strainer,
strain the drink into the cocktail glass and
serve.

SUGGESTED USE

A great drink to enjoy at all hours.

ALCOHOL CONTENT: 17.2
CALORIES: 184

JUS D'AMOUR BARBARA

Shake and Strain method

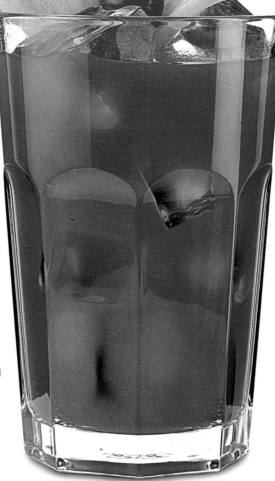

INGREDIENTS

white rum 1 oz (3cl)
Maraschino liqueur ¾ oz (2.5 cl)
pineapple juice 2½ oz (7.5 cl)
strawberry puree or strawberry juice
1 oz (3 cl)
grenadine syrup ½ oz (1.5 cl)

PREPARATION

Measure 1 oz (3 cl) of white rum in a
jigger and pour into a shaker. Repeat
with ¾ oz (2.5 cl) of Maraschino
liqueur, 2½ oz (7.5 cl) of pineapple
juice, 1 oz (3 cl) of strawberry juice or
strawberry puree, and ½ oz (1.5 cl) of
grenadine syrup. Add some ice cubes
and shake vigorously for a few seconds.
Holding the ice back with a strainer, strain
the drink into tall tumbler filled with ice
and serve, garnished with ½ a slice of
pineapple, 2 cocktail cherries, and 2 long
straws.

SUGGESTED USE

A drink especially suitable for women.

LISBONA BEACH

Shake and Strain method

ALCOHOL CONTENT: 11.8

CALORIES: 138

INGREDIENTS

White Port 1 oz (3 cl)
peach liqueur 1 oz (3 cl)
orange juice 2 oz (6 cl)
cranberry juice 2 oz (6 cl)

PREPARATION

Measure 1 oz (3 cl) of White Port,
1 oz (3 cl) of peach liqueur, 2 oz
(6 cl) of orange juice and
2 oz (6 cl) cranberry juice into
a jigger and pour into a shaker.
Add a few ice cubes and shake
vigorously. Holding the ice back with
a strainer, strain the drink into a tall
tumbler filled with ice. Serve with 2
long straws and garnish as desired
with a few wedges of citrus fruit and 1
sprig of red currants.

SUGGESTED USE

A very enjoyable drink that can refresh
any time of the day.

LONG ISLAND ICED TEA

Building method

INGREDIENTS

gin ¾ oz (2.5 cl)
light or amber rum ¾ oz (2.5 cl)
dry vodka ¾ oz (2.5 cl)
Cointreau or triple sec ¾ oz (2.5 cl)
lemon or lime juice ¾ oz (2.5 cl)
simple syrup ¾ oz (2.5 cl)
cola 1 oz (3 cl)

PREPARATION

In a jigger measure ¾ oz (2.5 cl) of light or amber rum and pour into a tumbler filled with ice. Repeat with ¾ oz (2.5 cl) of gin, ¾ oz (2.5 cl) of Cointreau or triple sec, ¾ oz (2.5 cl) of dry vodka, ¾ oz (2.5 cl) of lemon or lime juice, and ¾ oz (2.5 cl) of simple syrup. Add 1 oz (3 cl) of cola and mix the ingredients, stirring vigorously with a long-handled spoon for a few seconds. Serve, garnished with 2 long straws and ½ a slice of lime or lemon.

SUGGESTED USE

This drink is suitable for all hours of the day but is to be drunk responsibly, due to its high alcohol content.

LULÙ ICE

Blending method

ALCOHOL CONTENT: 14.2

CALORIES: 226

INGREDIENTS

Aperol 2 oz (6 cl)
bitter (Campari bitter is
recommended) ¾ oz
(2.5 cl)
Mandarinetto
Isolabella 1 oz (3 cl)
ACE (orange/carrot/
lemon) ice cream
5¼ oz (100 g) approx.

PREPARATION

Measure 2 oz (6 cl) of Aperol in a
jigger and pour into a blender. Repeat
with 1 oz (3 cl) of Mandarinetto
Isolabella and ¾ oz (2.5 cl) of bitter.
Add 5¼ oz (100 g) approximately
of ACE ice cream and ½ a low tumbler
of crushed ice. Blend for 15–20 seconds
and pour into a tall tumbler. Serve,
garnished with ½ a slice of orange,
1 cocktail cherry, and 2 long straws.

SUGGESTED USE

An excellent aperitif.

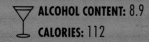
MADEIRA AMARETTO COLADA

Blending method

INGREDIENTS

sweet white Madeira 1 oz (3 cl)
Amaretto Disaronno 1 oz (3 cl)
coconut puree ½ oz (1.5 cl)
pineapple juice 3 oz (9 cl)

PREPARATION

Measure all the ingredients in a jigger
and pour everything into a blender.
Add ½ a tall tumbler of crushed ice
and blend for 15–20 seconds. Pour into
the tumbler and serve, garnished with
2 long straws, ½ a slice of pineapple,
2 cocktail cherries, and a few amaretto
cookies.

SUGGESTED USE

Great to enjoy at any time of the day.

MAI TAI

Shake and Strain method

ALCOHOL CONTENT: 18.6
CALORIES: 182

This 1997 movie, directed by the talented Gus Van Sant, secured a pair of friends, Matt Damon and Ben Affleck (winners of the Oscar for best original script), a place among the greatest movie stars of Hollywood. In one scene in this classic story of social redemption, the girlfriend of Will (Matt Damon) orders "another Mai Tai" in a bar. This tropical drink came back into fashion at the end of the '90s, thanks to this movie.

GOOD WILL HUNTING

INGREDIENTS
light rum 1½ oz (4.5 cl)
dark rum ¾ oz (2.5 cl)
lime or lemon juice ½ oz (1.5 cl)
Cointreau or triple sec ½ oz (1.5 cl)
orgeat syrup ½ oz (1.5 cl)

PREPARATION
Measure 1½ oz (4.5 cl) of light rum in a jigger and pour into a shaker. Repeat with ¾ oz (2.5 cl) of dark rum, ½ oz (1.5 cl) of Cointreau or triple sec, ½ oz (1.5 cl) of lime or lemon juice, and ½ oz (1.5 cl) of orgeat syrup. Add some ice cubes and shake vigorously for a few seconds. Holding the ice back with a strainer, strain the drink into a tall tumbler filled with ice and serve, garnished with ½ a slice of pineapple, 2 cocktail cherries, a nice sprig of fresh mint, and 2 long straws.

SUGGESTED USE
This long drink can be enjoyable at every moment of your day.

ALCOHOL CONTENT: 24.6
CALORIES: 172

MARY ANN

Shake and Strain method

INGREDIENTS

Rye, Canadian, or American whiskey
1½ oz (4.5 cl)
Amaretto Disaronno ¾ oz (2.5 cl)
Southern Comfort 1 oz (3 cl)

PREPARATION

Measure 1½ oz (4.5 cl) of whiskey
in a jigger and pour into a shaker.
Repeat with ¾ oz (2.5 cl) of Amaretto
Disaronno and 1 oz (3 cl) of Southern
Comfort. Add some ice cubes and shake
vigorously for a few seconds. Strain
the drink into a glass (pre-chilled in the
freezer), holding the ice back with the
strainer, and serve garnished with a
cocktail cherry.

SUGGESTED USE

A wonderful digestive cocktail, it is
recommended throughout the evening.

MERCEDES

Building method

INGREDIENTS

tequila 1 oz (3 cl)
Aperol 2 oz (6 cl)
strawberry smoothie or
puree 1 oz (3 cl)
grapefruit juice 2 oz (6 cl)

PREPARATION

Measure 1 oz (3 cl) of tequila in a
jigger and pour into a tall tumbler
filled with ice. Repeat with 2 oz (6
cl) of Aperol, 2 oz (6 cl) of grapefruit
juice, and 1 oz (3 cl) of strawberry
smoothie or puree. Stir vigorously for a
few seconds with a long-handled spoon
and serve, garnished with ½ a slice
of orange, 2 strawberries, and 2 long
straws.

SUGGESTED USE

An excellent aperitif to enjoy before a
Mexican meal.

ALCOHOL CONTENT: 16.3
CALORIES: 228

MINT JULEP

Building method

In a funny scene from this 1950 movie directed by Vincente Minnelli, an undisputed master of American comedy, Stanley (Spencer Tracy), the father of the bride, is busy preparing several Mint Juleps that the guests seem to really appreciate. The drink, which was little known up to that time, became very popular thanks to this movie.

INGREDIENTS
American whiskey 2 oz (6 cl)
white sugar 1 tbsp. (20 g) approx.
still water ¾ oz (2.5 cl)
fresh mint leaves ¼ oz (7 g) approx.
angostura 1 dash (2–3 drops)

PREPARATION
In a low tumbler place ¼ oz (7 g) approximately of fresh mint leaves. Add 1 tbsp. (20 g) approximately of white sugar, 1½ oz (4.5 cl) of American whiskey, and ¾ oz (2.5 cl) of still water (previously measured in a jigger). Stir with a long-handled spoon, trying to press the mint leaves against the sides of the tumbler. Fill with crushed (preferably) ice and finish with ½ oz (1.5 cl) of American whiskey previously measured in a jigger. Stir again with a spoon for a few seconds and serve, garnished with 2 long straws.

SUGGESTED USE
A great drink to enjoy throughout the day.

ORANGE SPICY MOJITO

Muddler method

ALCOHOL CONTENT: 11.2
CALORIES: 188

INGREDIENTS

light or amber
rum 2 oz (6 cl)
¼ fresh orange
white or cane sugar 1 tbsp.
(20 g) approx.
fresh ginger
ginger beer 2 oz (6 cl)
fresh mint ¼ oz (7 g) approx.

PREPARATION

Cut ¼ of an orange into cubes, put in
a tall tumbler, and add 1 tbsp. (20 g)
approximately of white or cane sugar.
Grind everything with a pestle until it is
pulp. Add a few slices of ginger and ¼ oz
(7 g) approximately of mint, gently pressing
it all against the glass. Fill with crushed ice
or ice cubes and add 2 oz (6 cl) of light or
amber rum (previously measured in a jigger).
Fill almost to the brim with 2 oz (6 cl) of ginger
beer and mix with a long-handled spoon
so that the ingredients blend well. To serve,
garnish with 1 nice sprig of fresh mint and 2
long straws.

SUGGESTED USE

An excellent drink for the evening that,
however, is becoming more and more
popular as an aperitif.

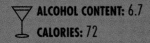

ALCOHOL CONTENT: 6.7
CALORIES: 72

ORIENTAL

Shake and Strain method

INGREDIENTS

dry Marsala 2 oz (6 cl)
lemon or lime juice 1 oz (3 cl)
simple syrup ½ oz (1.5 cl)

PREPARATION

Measure 2 oz (6 cl) of dry Marsala in
a jigger and pour into a shaker. Repeat
with 1 oz (3 cl) of lemon or lime juice
and ½ oz (1.5 cl) of simple syrup. Add
a few ice cubes and shake vigorously
for a few seconds. Holding the ice back
with a strainer, strain the drink into a
cocktail glass pre-chilled in the freezer
and serve.

SUGGESTED USE

Especially recommended as a digestif.

PALM BEACH

Shake and Strain method

INGREDIENTS

gin 1½ oz (4.5 cl)
bitter (Campari bitter is
recommended) 1½ oz (4.5 cl)
pineapple juice 3 oz (9 cl)

PREPARATION

Measure 1½ oz (4.5 cl) of gin in
a jigger and pour into a transparent
shaker. Repeat with 1½ oz (4.5 cl)
of bitter and 3 oz (9 cl) of pineapple
juice. Add ice cubes and shake
vigorously for a few seconds. Holding
the ice back with a strainer, strain the
drink into a tall tumbler filled with ice
and serve, garnished with ½ a slice of
pineapple, 2 cocktail cherries, and 2 long
straws.

SUGGESTED USE

Perfect as an aperitif.

ALCOHOL CONTENT: 10.5
CALORIES: 180

PIÑA COLADA

Blending method

INGREDIENTS

light rum 1½ oz (4.5 cl)
coconut puree 1 oz (3 cl)
pineapple juice 3 oz (9 cl)

PREPARATION

Measure 1½ oz (4.5 cl) of light rum in a jigger and transfer it to a blender. Repeat with 3 oz (9 cl) of pineapple juice and 1 oz (3 cl) of coconut puree. Add ½ a tall tumbler of crushed ice and blend everything for 15–20 seconds. Pour into the tumbler and serve, garnished with ½ a slice of pineapple, 2 cocktail cherries, and 2 long straws.

SUGGESTED USE

A tasty drink recommended for all hours of the day.

PINK LADY

Shake and Strain method

ALCOHOL CONTENT: 16.6
CALORIES: 172

INGREDIENTS

gin 1 oz (3 cl)
Cointreau or triple sec ¾ oz (2.5 cl)
lemon or lime juice ¾ oz (2.5 cl)
grenadine syrup ½ oz (1.5 cl)

PREPARATION

Measure 1 oz (3 cl) of gin in a jigger
and pour into a shaker. Repeat with ¾ oz
(2.5 cl) of Cointreau or triple sec, ¾ oz
(2.5 cl) of lemon or lime juice, and ½ oz
(1.5 cl) of grenadine syrup. Add a few
ice cubes and shake vigorously for a few
seconds. Strain the drink into a cocktail
glass (pre-cooled in the freezer), holding
the ice back with the strainer.

SUGGESTED USE

This is considered a purely evening drink.

ALCOHOL CONTENT: 6.4
CALORIES: 114

PINK ORANGE RED

Building method

INGREDIENTS

red vermouth 1 ½ oz (4.5 cl)
grapefruit juice 2 oz (6 cl)

PREPARATION

Measure 1 ½ oz (4.5 cl) of red vermouth in a jigger
and pour in a low tumbler filled with ice. Repeat
with 2 oz (6 cl) of grapefruit juice and stir with a
long-handled spoon. Serve garnished with 1 wedge
of orange, 1 cocktail cherry, 1 sprig of currants,
and 2 short straws.

SUGGESTED USE

A nice aperitif, but also excellent to enjoy at all
hours of the day.

PLANTER'S PUNCH

Shake and Strain method

ALCOHOL CONTENT: 12.2
CALORIES: 164

Among the most iconic movie characters of the last decades are the tyrannical Miranda Priestley (Meryl Streep) and the sweet Andrea Sachs (Anne Hathaway), who are the protagonists of this successful 2006 comedy. During a vernissage, bowls of Planter's Punch are offered to guests. Since then, this cocktail has become popular and has been associated with the elegance of the fashion world.

INGREDIENTS

dark rum 1½ oz (4.5 cl)
lemon or lime juice ¼ oz (0.75 cl)
orange juice 1¼ oz (4 cl)
pineapple juice 1¼ oz (4 cl)
grenadine syrup ¼ oz (0.75 cl)
simple syrup ¼ oz (0.75 cl)
angostura 1 dash (2–3 drops)

PREPARATION

Measure 1½ oz (4.5 cl) of dark rum in a jigger and pour into a shaker. Repeat with 1 ¼ oz (4 cl) of orange juice, 1¼ oz (4 cl) of pineapple juice, ¼ oz (0.75 cl) of lemon or lime juice, ¼ oz (0.75 cl) of grenadine syrup, ¼ oz (0.75 cl) of simple syrup, and a dash (2–3 drops) of angostura. Add some ice cubes and shake vigorously for a few seconds. Holding the ice back with a strainer, strain the drink into a tall tumbler filled with ice. Mix with a long-handled spoon and serve, garnished with an orange slice, 2 cocktail cherries, and 2 long straws.

SUGGESTED USE

A nice drink to enjoy freely at all hours of the day.

PORTO MOJITO

Muddler method

INGREDIENTS

White Port 1½ oz (4.5 cl)
white or cane sugar 1 tbsp. (20 g)
approx.
fresh mint ¼ oz (7 g) approx.
½ lime
sparkling water or soda water 2 oz (6 cl)

PREPARATION

Cut ½ a lime into small cubes and put
in a tall tumbler. Add 1 tbsp. (20 g)
approximately of white or cane sugar and
grind everything with a pestle until it is pulp.
Add ¼ oz (7 g) approximately of mint and
press it gently. Fill the glass with ice cubes
or crushed ice and add 1½ oz (4.5 cl) of
White Port, previously measured in a jigger.
Fill almost to the brim with 2 oz (6 cl) of
sparkling water or soda water. Stir for a few
seconds with a long-handled spoon. Serve
garnished with 2 long straws and 1 sprig of
fresh mint.

SUGGESTED USE

Excellent as an aperitif, but also great to enjoy
throughout the evening.

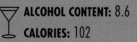
ALCOHOL CONTENT: 8.6
CALORIES: 102

PORTO WASSER

Building method

INGREDIENTS

raspberry puree ¾ oz (2.5 cl)
White Port 1 oz (3 cl)
sparkling water or soda water 4 oz
(12 cl)

PREPARATION

Measure ¾ oz (2.5 cl) of raspberry
puree in a jigger and pour into a tall
tumbler filled with ice. Repeat with 1
oz (3 cl) of White Port. Fill almost to
the brim with 4 oz (12 cl) of sparkling
water or soda water. Stir gently with a
long-handled spoon and serve garnished
with 2 long straws, ½ a wedge of
lemon, and 2 cocktail cherries.

SUGGESTED USE

A particularly thirst-quenching drink to
enjoy throughout the day.

ALCOHOL CONTENT: 6.6
CALORIES: 68

RED CAIPI PORTO

Muddler method

ALCOHOL CONTENT: 8.9
CALORIES: 98

INGREDIENTS
½ lime
white or cane sugar 1 tbsp.
(20 g) approx.
Ruby Port 2 oz (6 cl)

PREPARATION
Cut ½ a lime into small cubes
and put it in a low tumbler with 1
tbsp. (20 g) approximately of white
or cane sugar. Grind everything
with a pestle until it is pulp. Fill the
glass with ice cubes or crushed ice
and add 2 oz (6 cl) of Ruby Port,
previously measured in a jigger.
Stir for a few seconds with a long-
handled spoon so as to best mix all the
ingredients. Serve garnished with
2 short straws.

SUGGESTED USE
Excellent as an aperitif or at any other
time of the day.

RED PALM BEACH

Shake and Strain method

INGREDIENTS
Ruby Port 1 ½ oz (4.5 cl)
bitter (Campari bitter is
recommended) 1 oz (3 cl)
pineapple juice 3 oz (9 cl)

PREPARATION
Measure 1 ½ oz (4.5 cl) of Ruby Port
in a jigger and pour into a shaker.
Repeat with 1 oz (3 cl) of bitter and
3 oz (9 cl) of pineapple juice. Add
a few ice cubes and shake vigorously
for a few seconds. Holding the ice
back with a strainer, strain the drink into
a tall tumbler filled with ice and serve
garnished with 2 long straws, ½ a slice
of pineapple, and 2 cocktail cherries.

SUGGESTED USE
Excellent as an aperitif, but also
recommended for any other time
of the day.

ALCOHOL CONTENT: 12.2
CALORIES: 104

SEA BREEZE

Building method

INGREDIENTS
dry vodka 1 ½ oz (4.5 cl)
grapefruit juice 2 oz (6 cl)
cranberry juice 2 oz (6 cl)

PREPARATION
Measure 1 ½ oz (4.5 cl) of dry vodka
in a jigger and pour into a tall tumbler
filled with ice. Repeat with 2 oz (6 cl)
of grapefruit juice and 2 oz (6 cl) of
cranberry juice. Mix the ingredients well
with a long-handled spoon and serve,
garnished with 2 long straws and a slice of
lemon.

SUGGESTED USE
This long drink can be enjoyed at all hours
of the day.

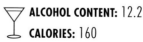

ALCOHOL CONTENT: 12.2
CALORIES: 160

The unforgettable protagonist of this 1992 remake is the former Lieutenant Colonel Frank Slade, masterfully played by the Oscar-winning Al Pacino. A great lover of beautiful women and sports cars, the protagonist goes blind and alternates between tantrums and moments of poetic nostalgia. During Thanksgiving, Frank tells his young assistant, Charlie Simms (Chris O'Donnell), how as a young man he used to drink Sea Breezes with friends.

ALCOHOL CONTENT: 12.2
CALORIES: 145

SEX ON THE BEACH

Shake and Strain method

INGREDIENTS

dry vodka 1 oz (3 cl)
peach liqueur 1 oz (3 cl)
orange juice 2 oz (6 cl)
cranberry juice 2 oz (6 cl)

PREPARATION

Pour 1 oz (3 cl) of dry vodka, 1 oz
(3 cl) of peach liqueur, 2 oz (6 cl)
of orange juice and 2 oz (6 cl) of
cranberry juice (previously measured in
a jigger) into a shaker. Add a few ice
cubes and shake vigorously. Holding the
ice back with a strainer, strain the drink
into a tall tumbler filled with ice. Serve,
adding 2 long straws, and garnish with
2 slices of citrus fruit to taste.

SUGGESTED USE

An excellent long drink to enjoy during the
hottest hours of the day.

SINGAPORE SLING
TWIST LIGHT

Shake and Strain method

ALCOHOL CONTENT: 14.3
CALORIES: 208

In 1988, Terry Gilliam directed this deranged adaptation of Hunter S. Thompson's novel. The protagonists are played by Johnny Depp and Benicio del Toro, who in this psychedelic road movie go wild abusing drugs and alcohol. The former constantly drinks Singapore Slings, often with the addition of Mezcal. Following the release of the movie, the Singapore Sling became beloved among cocktail and movies lovers.

FEAR AND LOATHING IN LAS VEGAS

INGREDIENTS

gin ¾ oz (2.5 cl)
cherry brandy ¾ oz (2.5 cl)
Cointreau or triple sec ¾ oz (2.5 cl)
grenadine syrup ¾ oz (2.5 cl)
lemon or lime juice ½ oz (1.5 cl)
soda or sparkling water 2 oz (6 cl)

PREPARATION

Measure ¾ oz (2.5 cl) of gin in a jigger and pour into a shaker with some ice. Repeat with ¾ oz (2.5 cl) of cherry brandy, ¾ oz (2.5 cl) of Cointreau or triple sec, ¾ oz (2.5 cl) of grenadine syrup, and ½ oz (1.5 cl) of lemon or lime juice. Shake vigorously for a few seconds then, holding the ice back with a strainer, strain the drink into a tall tumbler filled with ice. Fill almost to the brim with 2 oz (6 cl) of soda or sparkling water, then stir with a long-handled spoon. Serve, garnished with 2 long straws, ½ a slice of pineapple, and 2 cocktail cherries.

SUGGESTED USE

A long drink that can cheer you up at all hours of the day.

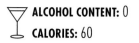 **ALCOHOL CONTENT:** 0
CALORIES: 60

SKIWASSER

Building method

INGREDIENTS

raspberry puree ½ oz (1.5 cl)
lemon or lime juice 1 oz (3 cl)
soda water or sparkling water 4 oz
(12 cl)

PREPARATION

Measure ½ oz (1.5 cl) of raspberry
puree in a jigger and pour into a tall
tumbler filled with ice. Repeat with 1
oz (3 cl) of lemon or lime juice, filling
almost to the brim with 4 oz (12 cl)
of soda or sparkling water. Stir gently
with a long-handled spoon and serve,
garnished with 2 long straws, ½ a slice
of lemon, and 2 cocktail cherries.

SUGGESTED USE

A great refreshing drink, this cocktail is
recommended throughout the summer.

TEQUILA SUNRISE

Building method

ALCOHOL CONTENT: 12.6
CALORIES: 160

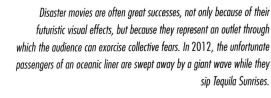

Disaster movies are often great successes, not only because of their futuristic visual effects, but because they represent an outlet through which the audience can exorcise collective fears. In 2012, the unfortunate passengers of an oceanic liner are swept away by a giant wave while they sip Tequila Sunrises.

2012

INGREDIENTS

tequila 1 ½ oz (4.5 cl)
orange juice 3 oz (9 cl)
grenadine syrup ½ oz (1.5 cl)

PREPARATION

Measure 1 ½ oz (4.5 cl) of tequila in a jigger and pour into a tall tumbler filled with ice. Repeat with 3 oz (9 cl) of orange juice. Stir with a long-handled spoon, then place it on the rim of the glass. Pour ½ oz (1.5 cl) of grenadine syrup (previously measured in a jigger) over the spoon, letting it slide slowly through the drink until it reaches the bottom of the tumbler, thus obtaining the rising sun effect. To serve, garnish with ½ an orange slice and 2 long straws.

SUGGESTED USE

One of the most visual and highly recommended long drinks in times of great heat.

TOM COLLINS

Building method

The grouchy Jack Byrnes, played by Robert De Niro in his first comic role, is one of the protagonists of this 2000 blockbuster comedy. There are three things that Jack cannot resist doing: exposing the scatterbrained suitor (Ben Stiller) of his daughter; pampering Jinx, the haughty family cat; and sipping a good Tom Collins, a drink he is crazy about.

INGREDIENTS

gin 1½ oz (4.5 cl)
lemon or lime juice ¾ oz (2.5 cl)
simple syrup ½ oz (1.5 cl)
soda water or sparkling water 2 oz
(6 cl)

PREPARATION

Measure 1½ oz (4.5 cl) of gin in a jigger and pour into a tall tumbler filled with ice. Repeat with ¾ oz (2.5 cl) of lemon or lime juice and ½ oz (1.5 cl) of simple syrup. Fill almost to the rim with 2 oz (6 cl) of soda water or sparkling water. Mix everything together with a long-handled spoon and serve, garnished with slices of lemon, 2 cocktail cherries, and 2 long straws.

SUGGESTED USE

Excellent thirst-quenching drink, suitable for any time of the day.

TURQUOISE BLUE

Shake and Strain method

ALCOHOL CONTENT: 16.6
CALORIES: 152

This movie par excellence about the world of cocktails stars a very young Tom Cruise as Brian Flanagan, an ambitious and entertaining bartender. The Turquoise Blue is one of the numerous drinks that the young man prepares in this 1988 movie, which defined a generation and inspired bartenders all over the world, introducing the spectacular "flair bartending" into the popular imagination.

COCKTAIL

INGREDIENTS

light rum ¾ oz (2.5 cl)
Cointreau or triple sec ¾ oz (2.5 cl)
Blue Curaçao ¾ oz (2.5 cl)
pineapple juice 3 oz (9 cl)
lemon or lime juice ½ oz (1.5 cl)

PREPARATION

Measure ¾ oz (2.5 cl) of light rum in a jigger and pour into a shaker. Repeat with ¾ oz (2.5 cl) of Cointreau or triple sec, ¾ oz (2.5 cl) of Blue Curaçao, 3 oz (9 cl) of pineapple juice, and ½ oz (1.5 cl) of lemon or lime juice. Add a few ice cubes and shake vigorously for a few seconds. Holding the ice back with a strainer, strain the drink into a tall tumbler filled with ice and serve, garnished with ½ a slice of pineapple, 2 cocktail cherries, and 2 long straws.

SUGGESTED USE

This long drink is perfect for every hour of the day.

VERMOUTH FRUITS

Building method

INGREDIENTS
dry vermouth 1¼ oz (4 cl)
orange juice 2 oz (6 cl)
grapefruit juice 2 oz (6 cl)

PREPARATION
Measure 1¼ oz (4 cl) of dry vermouth
in a jigger and pour into a tall tumbler
filled with ice. Repeat with 2 oz (6
cl) of orange juice and 2 oz (6 cl) of
grapefruit juice. Stir with a long-handled
spoon and serve garnished with 1 slice
of pineapple and 1 cocktail cherry.

SUGGESTED USE
An excellent citrus aperitif. Nice to enjoy
throughout the day.

ALCOHOL CONTENT: 9.7
CALORIES: 57

Tony Montana (Al Pacino) and Manny Ribera (Steven Bauer) are the two Cuban gangster protagonists of this 1980 film noir directed by Brian De Palma. While planning their accession in Miami, they enjoy several tasty Caribbean drinks, among which the Virgin Colada stands out. After Scarface, serving this drink directly in hollowed-out fruit, like a coconut or melon, came back into fashion.

VIRGIN COLADA
(PIÑITA COLADA)

Blending method

INGREDIENTS

pineapple juice 4 oz (12 cl)
coconut puree 1 oz (3 cl)
cream ¾ oz (2.5 cl)

PREPARATION

Measure 4 oz (12 cl) of pineapple juice in a jigger and pour into a blender. Repeat with ¾ oz (2.5 cl) of cream and 1 oz (3 cl) of coconut puree. Add ½ a tall tumbler of crushed ice and blend for 15–20 seconds. Pour into the tumbler and serve, garnished with ¼ a slice of pineapple, 2 cocktail cherries, and 2 long straws.

SUGGESTED USE

A tasty and energy-boosting, non-alcoholic long drink that is also recommended in the morning for breakfast.

ALCOHOL CONTENT: 0
CALORIES: 234

VIRGIN MOJITO

Muddler method

INGREDIENTS
½ lime
fresh mint ¼ oz (7 g) approx.
white or cane sugar 1 tbsp. (20 g) approx.
lemon soft drink or ginger ale 4 oz (12 cl)

PREPARATION
Put ½ a lime, cut into cubes, in a tall tumbler and add 1 tbsp. (20 g) approximately of white or cane sugar. Grind everything with a pestle until it is pulp. Add ¼ oz (7 g) approximately of fresh mint and press lightly against the glass. Fill with crushed ice or ice cubes and fill to the brim with 4 oz (12 cl) of lemon soft drink or ginger ale (previously measured in a jigger). Mix everything with a long-handled spoon so that the ingredients blend well. To serve, garnish with 1 sprig of fresh mint and 2 long straws.

SUGGESTED USE
A refreshing drink that can be enjoyed throughout the evening, it is also suitable for the very young.

WHISKEY COBBLER

Building method

ALCOHOL CONTENT: 12.8

CALORIES: 172

INGREDIENTS

American whiskey 1½ oz (4.5 cl)
grenadine syrup ½ oz (1.5 cl)
ginger ale 2 oz (6 cl)
fresh fruit of the season 2 oz (60 g)
approx.

PREPARATION

Measure 1½ oz (4.5 cl) of whiskey in
a jigger and pour into a tall tumbler.
Repeat with ½ oz (1.5 cl) of grenadine
syrup and 2 oz (6 cl) of ginger ale.
Add 2 oz (60 g) approximately of fresh
seasonal fruit, then fill almost to the
brim with crushed ice. Stir with a long-
handled spoon and serve, garnished
with 1 long toothpick and 2 long straws.

SUGGESTED USE

A low-alcohol and very festive long drink.
Great to be enjoyed at all hours of the day.

WHITE WINE MOJITO

Muddler method

INGREDIENTS

Vermentino wine 2 oz (6 cl)
white or cane sugar 1 tbsp.
(20 g) approx.
fresh mint ¼ oz (7 g) approx.
½ lime
sparkling water or soda water 2 oz (6 cl)

PREPARATION

Cut ½ a lime into small cubes and put
in a tall tumbler. Add 1 tbsp. (20 g)
approximately of white or cane sugar
and grind everything with a pestle until it
is pulp. Add ¼ oz (7 g) approximately
of fresh mint leaves, gently pressing
them. Fill the glass with crushed ice
or ice cubes and add 2 oz (6 cl) of
Vermentino wine previously measured
in a jigger, then fill almost to the brim
with 2 oz (6 cl) of sparkling water or
soda water previously measured in
a jigger. Stir for a few seconds with
a long-handled spoon and serve,
garnished with 2 long straws and 1
sprig of fresh mint.

SUGGESTED USE

A great refreshing aperitif.

ALCOHOL CONTENT: 6.8
CALORIES: 168

WHISKEY SLING

Building method

INGREDIENTS

American whiskey 1½ oz
(4.5 cl)
white sugar 1 tbsp. (20 g)
approx.
lemon or lime juice 1 oz (3 cl)
soda water or sparkling water
3 oz (9 cl)

PREPARATION

Measure 1½ oz (4.5 cl) of whiskey
in a jigger and pour into a tall
tumbler filled with ice. Repeat with 1
oz (3 cl) of lemon or lime juice. Add
1 tbsp. (20 g) approximately of white
sugar and fill almost to the brim of the
glass with 3 oz (9 cl) of soda water or
sparkling mineral water. Stir for a few
seconds with a long-handled spoon and
serve, garnished with 2 cocktail cherries,
½ a slice of lemon, and 2 long straws.

SUGGESTED USE

A long drink suitable for any time of the
day or evening.

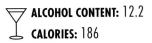

ALCOHOL CONTENT: 12.2
CALORIES: 186

WILD RED

Building method

INGREDIENTS
red vermouth ¾ oz (2.5 cl)
dry vodka 1¼ oz (4 cl)
berry juice 1 oz (3 cl)
lemon or lime juice 1 oz (3 cl)
lemon-flavored soft drink 1 oz (3 cl)

PREPARATION
Measure ¾ oz (2.5 cl) of red vermouth in a jigger and pour into a tall tumbler filled with ice. Repeat with 1¼ oz (4 cl) of dry vodka, 1 oz (3 cl) of berry juice, 1 oz (3 cl) of lemon or lime juice and 1 oz (3 cl) of lemon-flavored soft drink. Stir with a long-handled spoon and serve garnished with some berries.

SUGGESTED USE
A tasty and thirst-quenching aperitif to enjoy throughout the day.

ALCOHOL CONTENT: 12.6
CALORIES: 148

WINE LEMON

Building method

INGREDIENTS
Pinot Gris wine 1½ oz (4.5 cl)
lemon soft drink 4 oz (12 cl)

PREPARATION
Measure 1½ oz (4.5 cl) of Pinot Gris wine in a jigger and pour into a tall tumbler filled with ice. Fill almost to the brim with 4 oz (12 cl) of lemon soft drink and serve garnished with 2 long straws, a few twists of lemon peel, and some white grapes.

SUGGESTED USE
A thirst-quenching drink, ideal to enjoy at any time of the day.

ALCOHOL CONTENT: 6.5
CALORIES: 72

ALCOHOL CONTENT: 6.8
CALORIES: 98

WINE MULE

Building method

INGREDIENTS

Terre di Franciacorta white wine
1 ½ oz (4.5 cl)
ginger beer 3 oz (9 cl)

PREPARATION

Measure 1 ½ oz (4.5 cl) of Terre di
Franciacorta white wine in a jigger
and pour into a low tumbler or a tin
mug filled with ice. Repeat with
3 oz (9 cl) of ginger beer. Stir for
a few seconds with a long-handled
spoon and serve garnished with 2 lime
wedges and a few white grapes cut in
half.

SUGGESTED USE

An excellent aperitif, enjoyable
throughout the day.

ZOMBIE

Shake and Pour or Blending method

ALCOHOL CONTENT: 24.8
CALORIES: 246

INGREDIENTS

light rum 1½ oz (4.5 cl)
dark rum 1½ oz (4.5 cl)
dark rum 75% vol. 1 oz (3 cl)
lime juice 1 oz (3 cl)
grapefruit juice ½ oz (1.5 cl)
cinnamon syrup ½ oz (1.5 cl)
Falernum syrup ½ oz (1.5 cl)
angostura 1 drop
Pernod 1 dash (5–6 drops)
grenadine syrup ¼ oz (0.75 cl)

PREPARATION

Measure 1½ oz (4.5 cl) of light rum in a
jigger and pour into a blender or a shaker.
Repeat with 1½ oz (4.5 cl) of dark rum,
1 oz (3 cl) of lime juice, ½ oz (1.5 cl) of
grapefruit juice, ½ oz (1.5 cl) of cinnamon
syrup, ½ oz (1.5 cl) of Falernum syrup,
and ¼ oz (0.75 cl) of grenadine syrup.
Add 1 drop of angostura and 1 dash
(5–6 drops) of Pernod and shake or blend
for a few seconds with no ice. Pour into
a tall tumbler or a tiki mug filled with ice,
preferably crushed. Finally, measure
1 oz (3 cl) of dark rum 75 % vol. in
a jigger and pour it gently into the glass
with a teaspoon so that it remains on the
surface.

SUGGESTED USE

A long drink very popular among younger
generations. Enjoy in moderation.

HAPPY HOUR
COCKTAILS

The practice of the Happy Hour was born in England in the early '80s when London pubs started serving two drinks for the price of one during a specific time frame. The British were enthusiastic and confirmed the success of the Happy Hour.

Nowadays, the Happy Hour has significantly evolved. In the early years, beer and single-serving aperitifs used to dominate the scene, but cocktails quickly became the undisputed protagonists.

Dry aperitifs, with a rather high alcohol content and served in a glass, have given way over the years to more flavored drinks with the addition of fragrant and sweet liqueurs (e.g., Peach Tree, Cointreau, Mandarinetto Isolabella) and fruit juices, from the most classical (e.g., orange, grapefruit, pineapple) to the most exotic (e.g., cranberry, maracuja, passion fruit). The use of sparkling soft drinks such as cola, tonic, or soda water helped decrease the alcohol content of these drinks.

Also with regard to culinary delights, the Happy Hour has had a natural evolution. Initially, the offer was limited to peanuts, potato chips, and pickles, but nowadays it is increasingly diversified, from nice finger food to proper warm dishes.

The time frame for the Happy Hour has changed from an inflexible one, between 5 p.m. and 6:30 p.m., to a more ample one, from 7 p.m. to 10 p.m., thus encouraging people to get together and relax.

In South America, whiskies and spirits like rum, pisco, or cachaça are very popular, whereas in France, Champagnes, dry white wines, or such liqueurs as the Pastis, the Ricard, or the Kir and its variants are preferred. The Spanish accompany sherry wines or beer with the traditional tapas. The British remain tied to the traditional beer, but they also appreciate Port wines and the Gin and Tonic, which has turned into a classic all over Europe in the last decade. Here, gin bars specializing in the blending of gin and tonic water have become a widespread success. The Americans remain the fans par excellence of blended drinks. Finally, in Italy, the Happy Hour has invested a great deal in culinary delights, with them even becoming fully fledged alternatives to dinner.

HAPPY HOUR COCKTAILS

50

NGREDIENTS
dry Marsala 2 oz (6 cl)
elderflower syrup 1 oz (3 cl)
sparkling water or soda water 2 oz
6 cl)

PREPARATION
Measure 2 oz (6 cl) of dry Marsala
in a jigger and pour into a wine glass
with a few ice cubes. Repeat with
1 oz (3 cl) of elderflower syrup and
2 oz (6 cl) of sparkling water or soda
water. Stir gently for a few seconds
with a long-handled spoon and serve
garnished with 1 lemon slice, 1 sprig of
mint, and a few white grapes cut in half.

SUGGESTED USE
Excellent as an aperitif, but also great to
enjoy at all hours.

ADONIS
Shake and Strain method

INGREDIENTS
dry sherry 2 oz (6 cl)
red vermouth 1 oz (3 cl)
orange bitter or Cointreau 1 dash (2–3
drops)

PREPARATION
Measure 2 oz (6 cl) of dry sherry in a
jigger and pour into a shaker. Repeat
with 1 oz (3 cl) of red vermouth and 1
dash (2–3 drops) of orange bitters or
Cointreau. Add a few ice cubes and
shake vigorously for a few seconds.
Holding the ice back with a strainer,
strain the drink into a cocktail cup
pre-chilled in the freezer and serve
garnished with some orange peel.

SUGGESTED USE
Excellent as an aperitif, but greatly
enjoyable throughout the evening
as well.

ALCOHOL CONTENT: 6.8
CALORIES: 62

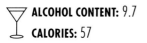

ALCOHOL CONTENT: 9.7
CALORIES: 57

AMERICANO

Building method

INGREDIENTS

bitter (Campari bitter is recommended) 1 oz (3 cl)
red vermouth 1 oz (3 cl)
soda water or sparkling water 1 oz (3 cl)

PREPARATION

Measure 1 oz (3 cl) of bitter in a jigger and pour in a low tumbler filled with ice. Repeat with 1 oz (3 cl) of red vermouth. Fill almost to the brim with 1 oz (3 cl) of soda water or sparkling water. Gently stir everything with a long-handled spoon and serve, garnished with ½ a slice of orange and some lemon peel (you can also gently spray the drink with the oil emanating from the citrus peel).

SUGGESTED USE

Excellent as an aperitif.

APEROL BIT ORANGE

Shake and Strain method

ALCOHOL CONTENT: 12.6
CALORIES: 97

INGREDIENTS

Aperol 1½ oz (4.5 cl)
bitter (Campari bitter is recommended)
½ oz (1.5 cl)
orange juice 3 oz (9 cl)
Mandarinetto Isolabella 1 oz (3 cl)

PREPARATION

Measure 1½ oz (4.5 cl) of Aperol in a jigger and pour in a shaker. Repeat with 3 oz (9 cl) of orange juice, ½ oz (1.5 cl) of bitter and 1 oz (3 cl) of Mandarinetto Isolabella. Shake vigorously for a few seconds, then, holding the ice back with a strainer, strain the drink into a tall tumbler filled with ice. To serve, garnish with ½ an orange slice, ½ a slice of grapefruit, ½ a slice of lime, and 2 long straws.

SUGGESTED USE

An excellent aperitif, it can also be enjoyed at all hours of the day.

ALCOHOL CONTENT: 9.8
CALORIES: 96

APEROL CRODO

Shake and Strain method

INGREDIENTS

Aperol 1 oz (3 cl)
peach liqueur ¾ oz (2.5 cl)
bitter (Campari bitter is
recommended) ½ oz (1.5 cl)
Crodino 3 oz (9 cl)

PREPARATION

Measure 1 oz (3 cl) of Aperol in a
jigger and pour into a shaker. Repeat
with ¾ oz (2.5 cl) of peach liqueur
and ½ oz (1.5 cl) of bitter. Shake
for a few seconds, then, holding the
ice back with a strainer, strain the
drink into a tall tumbler filled with ice.
Fill almost to the brim with 3 oz (9
cl) of Crodino. Gently stir and serve,
garnished with ½ a slice of orange,
3 small cubes of lime, 2 cocktail
cherries, and 2 long straws.

SUGGESTED USE

Great for happy hour, this drink is also
excellent to enjoy at all hours of the day.

APPLE MOJITO

Muddler method

INGREDIENTS

apple liqueur 2 oz (6 cl)
fresh mint ¼ oz (7 g) approx.
½ lime
white or cane sugar 1 tbsp. (20 g)
approx.
soda water or sparkling water 2 oz
(6 cl)

PREPARATION

Cut ½ a lime into cubes. Put the lime
cubes in a tall tumbler and add
1 tbsp. (20 g) approximately of white
or cane sugar. Grind everything with
a pestle until it is pulp. Add ¼ oz (7 g)
approximately of fresh mint and press
lightly. Fill the glass with crushed ice or
ice cubes and add 2 oz (6 cl) of apple
liqueur (previously measured in a jigger).
Fill almost to the brim with 2 oz (6 cl) of
soda water or sparkling water, then mix
with a long-handled spoon so that the
ingredients blend well. To serve, garnish
with nice sprigs of fresh mint and 2 long
straws.

SUGGESTED USE

A drink that can be enjoyed throughout
the evening.

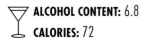

ALCOHOL CONTENT: 6.8
CALORIES: 72

BEETHOVEN

Building method

INGREDIENTS

wild berry puree 1½ oz (4.5 cl)
brut sparkling wine or Champagne 4 oz
(12 cl)

PREPARATION

Measure 1½ oz (4.5 cl) of wild
berry puree in a jigger (take some
blackberries, raspberries, and
blueberries and grind everything until it is
pulp). Pour into a glass or a wine glass
pre-chilled in the freezer. Fill almost to
the brim with 4 oz (12 cl) of well-chilled
brut sparkling wine or Champagne. Stir
gently with a long-handled spoon and
serve, garnished with some currants.

SUGGESTED USE

Perfect to enjoy at all hours of the day.

BELLINI

Building method

ALCOHOL CONTENT: 5.5
CALORIES: 48

Among the world's most appreciated aperitifs, the Bellini was created in 1948 at Harry's Bar in Venice to honor the painter Giovanni Bellini. This drink is mentioned in the second installment of the movie saga starring the fearless secret agent Ethan Hunt (Tom Cruise). Thanks to the great success of this 2000 movie, this delicate peach-flavored drink became surprisingly widespread all over the United States.

MISSION IMPOSSIBLE 2

INGREDIENTS

peach smoothie 1½ oz (4.5 cl)
brut sparkling wine or Champagne
4 oz (12 cl)

PREPARATION

Measure 1½ oz (4.5 cl) of peach smoothie in a jigger and pour into a cup or a wine glass pre-chilled in the freezer. Fill almost to the brim with 4 oz (12 cl) of well-chilled brut sparkling wine or Champagne. Stir gently with a long-handled spoon and serve.

SUGGESTED USE

An excellent aperitif.

BITTER MOJITO

Muddler method

INGREDIENTS

bitter (Campari bitter is recommended) 1½ oz (4.5 cl)
¼ fresh orange
white or cane sugar 1 tbsp. (20 g) approx.
brut sparkling wine 3 oz (9 cl)
fresh mint ¼ oz (7 g) approx.

PREPARATION

Cut ¼ of an orange into cubes. Put the orange cubes in a tall tumbler and add 1 tbsp. (20 g) approximately of white or cane sugar. Grind everything with a pestle until it is pulp. Add ¼ oz (7 g) approximately of fresh mint and press lightly. Fill the glass with crushed ice or ice cubes and add 1½ oz (4.5 cl) of bitter (previously measured in a jigger). Fill almost to the brim with 3 oz (9 cl) of fresh brut sparkling wine (previously measured in a jigger) and mix everything with a long-handled spoon so that the ingredients blend well. To serve, garnish with 1 nice sprig of fresh mint and 2 long straws.

SUGGESTED USE

Excellent as an aperitif.

BOMBAY

Shake and Strain method

ALCOHOL CONTENT: 18.6
CALORIES: 156

INGREDIENTS

cognac or brandy ¾ oz (2.5 cl)
dry vermouth 1 oz (3 cl)
red vermouth ¾ oz (2.5 cl)
Cointreau or triple sec ¾ oz (2.5 cl)
Pernod or Ricard ⅙ oz (0.5 cl)

PREPARATION

Measure ¾ oz (2.5 cl) of cognac or
brandy in a jigger and pour into a shaker.
Repeat with 1 oz (3 cl) of dry vermouth,
¾ oz (2.5 cl) of red vermouth, ¾ oz
(2.5 cl) of Cointreau or triple sec, and
⅙ oz (0.5 cl) of Pernod or Ricard. Add
a few ice cubes and shake vigorously for
a few seconds. Strain the drink into a cup
(pre-chilled in the freezer), holding the ice
back with the strainer, and serve.

SUGGESTED USE

Excellent as an aperitif, but extremely
enjoyable during the evening as well.

BOULEVARDIER

Stir and Strain method

INGREDIENTS

bourbon whiskey 1 oz (3 cl)
red vermouth 1 oz (3 cl)
bitter (Campari bitter is
recommended) 1 oz (3 cl)

PREPARATION

Measure 1 oz (3 cl) of bourbon
whiskey in a jigger and pour into a
mixing glass. Repeat with 1 oz (3 cl) of
red vermouth and 1 oz (3 cl) of bitter.
Add a few ice cubes then stir everything
with a long-handled spoon. Holding the
ice back with a strainer, strain the drink
into a cocktail glass previously chilled in
the freezer and serve, garnished with 2
cocktail cherries.

SUGGESTED USE

An excellent aperitif.

BRONX

Shake and Strain method

ALCOHOL CONTENT: 16.2
CALORIES: 126

INGREDIENTS

gin 1 oz (3 cl)
red vermouth ¾ oz (2.5 cl)
dry vermouth ½ oz (1.5 cl)
orange juice ¾ oz (2.5 cl)

PREPARATION

Measure 1 oz (3 cl) of gin in a jigger
and pour in a shaker. Repeat with ¾
oz (2.5 cl) of red vermouth, ½ oz (1.5
cl) of dry vermouth, and ¾ oz (2.5 cl)
of orange juice. Add some ice cubes
and shake vigorously for a few seconds.
Strain the drink into a glass (previously
chilled in the freezer), holding the ice
back with the strainer, and serve.

SUGGESTED USE

Perfect to drink at happy hour.

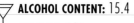

CANNES
Shake and Strain method

INGREDIENTS

brandy or cognac ¾ oz (2.5 cl)
dry vermouth 1 oz (3 cl)
bitter (Campari Bitter is recommended)
½ oz (1.5 cl)
orange juice 1 oz (3 cl)

PREPARATION

Measure ¾ oz (2.5 cl) of cognac or brandy in a jigger and pour into a shaker. Repeat with 1 oz (3 cl) of dry vermouth, ½ oz (1.5 cl) of bitter, and 1 oz (3 cl) of orange juice. Add some ice cubes and shake vigorously for a few seconds. Strain the drink into a glass (previously chilled in the freezer) and serve garnished with ½ an orange slice and 2 cocktail cherries.

SUGGESTED USE

Perfect as an aperitif.

CARDINALE

Stir and Strain method

INGREDIENTS

gin 1½ oz (4.5 cl)
bitter (Campari Bitter is recommended)
½ oz (1.5 cl)
dry vermouth ¾ oz (2.5 cl)

PREPARATION

Measure 1½ oz (4.5 cl) of gin in a
jigger and pour into a mixing glass.
Repeat with ¾ oz (2.5 cl) of dry
vermouth and ½ oz (1.5 cl) of bitter.
Add a few ice cubes and stir with a long-
handled spoon for a few seconds. Strain
the drink into a cocktail glass (previously
chilled in the freezer), holding the ice
back with the strainer.

SUGGESTED USE

Perfect as an aperitif.

ALCOHOL CONTENT: 13.6

CALORIES: 152

CASABLANCA

Set during the Second World War, Casablanca remains a romantic movie par excellence, where a man sacrifices his happiness to save his sweetheart. Humphrey Bogart and Ingrid Bergman are unforgettable. The legendary Rick's Café Américain, with its background piano music, is a crossroads of uncertain fates and illegal trafficking, and also showcases several drinks like the Champagne Cocktail. This drink, which had been considered niche up to that time, became famous thanks to this 1942 gem.

CHAMPAGNE COCKTAIL

Building method

INGREDIENTS

brandy or cognac ½ oz (1.5 cl)
Champagne or brut sparkling wine
(traditional method) 3 oz (9 cl)
sugar 1 lump
Grand Marnier ½ oz (1.5 cl)
angostura 1 dash (2–3 drops)

PREPARATION

Place 1 lump of sugar moistened with a
dash (2–3 drops) of angostura in a glass
or wine glass (pre-chilled in the freezer).
Add ½ oz (1.5 cl) of cognac or brandy
and ½ oz (1.5 cl) of Grand Marnier
(previously measured in a jigger). Repeat
with 3 oz (9 cl) of well-chilled Champagne
or brut sparkling wine. Mix gently with a
long-handled spoon and serve garnished with
½ an orange slice and a cocktail cherry.

SUGGESTED USE

A refined drink to enjoy as an aperitif but
perfect at any time.

CONTE DOURO

Building method

INGREDIENTS

gin 1 oz (3 cl)
Ruby Port 1 oz (3 cl)
bitter (Campari bitter is recommended) 1 oz
(3 cl)

PREPARATION

Measure 1 oz (3 cl) of gin in a jigger and
pour into a low tumbler filled with ice.
Repeat with 1 oz (3 cl) of Ruby Port and
1 oz (3 cl) of bitter. Stir for a few seconds
with a long-handled spoon and serve
garnished with ½ an orange slice.

SUGGESTED USE

A great alternative to the classic
Negroni.

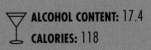 **ALCOHOL CONTENT:** 17.4
CALORIES: 118

DIRTY MARTINI

Stir and Strain method

IRON MAN

Iron Man was a resounding success in 2008 and the precursor of numerous blockbuster movies based on Marvel Comics characters, such as The Avengers, Thor, and Captain America. In this action movie, the fascinating Tony Stark (Robert Downey Jr.) orders two Dirty Martinis during a party—one for himself and the other for his beautiful girlfriend, Pepper Potts (Gwyneth Paltrow). The cocktail benefited from the success of Iron Man, becoming popular among fashionable drink lovers.

INGREDIENTS
dry vodka 2 oz (6 cl)
dry vermouth ½ oz (1.5 cl)
olive brine ⅙ oz (0.5 cl)

PREPARATION
Measure 2 oz (6 cl) of dry vodka in a jigger and pour into a mixing glass. Repeat with ½ oz (1.5 cl) of dry vermouth and ⅙ oz (0.5 cl) of olive brine, and add several ice cubes. Stir with a long-handled spoon then, holding the ice back with a strainer, strain the drink into a cocktail glass previously chilled in the freezer. Serve, garnished with 3–4 green olives on a skewer (be sure to rinse them well under running water to remove the brine) and a lemon peel twist.

SUGGESTED USE
An elegant aperitif with a strong character.

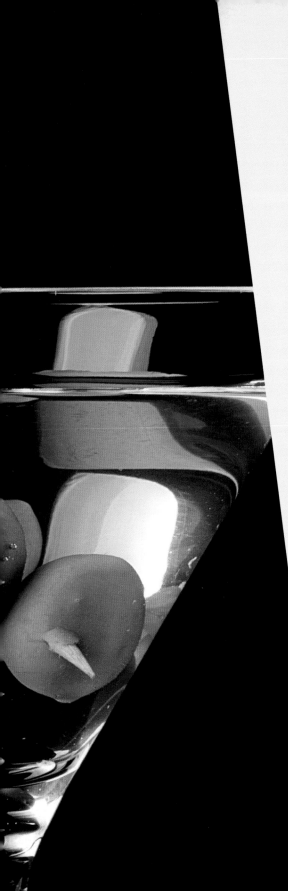

EVERYDAY
Building method

INGREDIENTS
white vermouth 1½ oz (4.5 cl)
bitter (Campari bitter is recommended) ½ oz
(1.5 cl)
dry vodka 1 oz (3 cl)

PREPARATION
Measure 1½ oz (4.5 cl) of white vermouth
in a jigger and pour into a low tumbler
filled with ice. Repeat with ½ oz (1.5 cl)
of bitter and 1 oz (3 cl) of dry vodka.
Stir gently for a few seconds with a
long-handled spoon and serve garnished
with 2 short straws and ½ a wedge of
orange.

SUGGESTED USE
An excellent aperitif with a sweet taste.

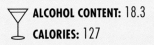
ALCOHOL CONTENT: 18.3
CALORIES: 127

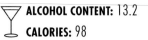

ALCOHOL CONTENT: 13.2
CALORIES: 98

GARIBALDI

Building method

INGREDIENTS

bitter (Campari bitter is
recommended) 2 oz (6 cl)
orange juice (preferably blood
orange juice) 3 oz (9 cl)

PREPARATION

Measure 2 oz (6 cl) of bitter in
a jigger and pour into a tall tumbler
filled with ice. Repeat with 3 oz (9 cl)
of orange juice. Stir for a few seconds
with a long-handled spoon and serve,
garnished with 1 orange wedge and
2 long straws.

SUGGESTED USE

A delicious aperitif, but also ideal to enjoy
at all hours of the day.

GAS-BAG

Shake and Strain method

INGREDIENTS

dry vodka ¾ oz (2.5 cl)
strawberry puree or smoothie 1 oz (3 cl)
bitter (Campari bitter is recommended)
½ oz (1.5 cl)
brut sparkling wine or Champagne
2 oz (6 cl)

PREPARATION

Measure ¾ oz (2.5 cl) of dry vodka in
a jigger and pour into a shaker. Repeat
with 1 oz (3 cl) of strawberry puree or
smoothie and ½ oz (1.5 cl) of bitter. Add
a few ice cubes and shake vigorously for
a few seconds. Holding the ice back with
a strainer, strain the drink into a cup or a
wine glass and fill almost to the brim with
2 oz (6 cl) of well-chilled brut sparkling
wine or Champagne. Stir gently and
serve.

SUGGESTED USE

An excellent aperitif, ideal to enjoy at all
hours of the day.

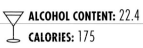

IBERICA

Stir and Strain method

INGREDIENTS

Canadian whiskey 2 oz (6 cl)
Ruby Port 1 oz (3 cl)
angostura 1 dash (2–3 drops)

PREPARATION

Measure 2 oz (6 cl) of Canadian whiskey
in a jigger and pour into a mixing glass.
Repeat with 1 oz (3 cl) of Ruby Port. Add 1
dash (2–3 drops) of angostura and a few
ice cubes. Stir with a long-handled spoon
then, holding the ice back with a strainer,
strain the drink into a cocktail glass pre-
chilled in the freezer. Serve garnished
with 1–2 cocktail cherries.

SUGGESTED USE

A great aperitif to enjoy as an
alternative to the Manhattan.

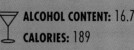 **ALCOHOL CONTENT:** 16.7
CALORIES: 189

GIN & IT

Stir and Strain method

INGREDIENTS

gin 2 oz (6 cl)
red vermouth 1 oz (3 cl)

PREPARATION

Measure 2 oz (6 cl) of gin in a jigger
and pour into a mixing glass. Repeat
with 1 oz (3 cl) of red vermouth. Add
some ice cubes and mix with a long-
handled spoon. Strain the drink into
a glass (previously chilled in the freezer),
holding the ice back with the strainer,
and serve.

SUGGESTED USE

Excellent as an aperitif.

ITALIA-CILE
(ITALY-CHILE)

Shake and Strain method

INGREDIENTS

Aperol 1 oz (3 cl)
bitter (Campari bitter is
recommended) ½ oz (1.5 cl)
pisco 1 oz (3 cl)
pineapple juice 1 oz (3 cl)

PREPARATION

Measure 1 oz (3 cl) of pisco in
a jigger and pour into a shaker.
Repeat with 1 oz (3 cl) of Aperol,
½ oz (1.5 cl) of bitter, and 1 oz (3
cl) of pineapple juice. Add some
ice cubes and shake vigorously for
a few seconds. Holding the ice back
with a strainer, strain the drink into a
low tumbler filled with ice and serve,
garnished with ½ an orange slice,
½ a slice of pineapple, 2 cocktail
cherries, and 2 short straws.

SUGGESTED USE

Excellent as an aperitif, but also good to
enjoy at all hours of the day.

ITALIAN BITTER

Shake and Strain method

ALCOHOL CONTENT: 8.2
CALORIES: 96

INGREDIENTS

Aperol 1 oz (3 cl)
bitter (Campari bitter is
recommended) ½ oz (1.5 cl)
peach liqueur ¾ oz (2.5 cl)
Sanbittèr 3 oz (9 cl)

PREPARATION

Measure 1 oz (3 cl) of Aperol in
a jigger and pour into a shaker.
Repeat with ¾ oz (2.5 cl) of peach
liqueur and ½ oz (1.5 cl) of bitter.
Shake for a few seconds, then,
holding the ice back with a strainer,
strain the drink into a tall tumbler filled
with ice. Fill almost to the brim with
3 oz (9 cl) of Sanbittèr and stir gently
with long-handled spoon. Serve,
garnished with ½ a slice of orange,
2 cocktail cherries, and 2 long straws.

SUGGESTED USE

Excellent as an aperitif.

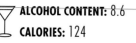
KIR ROYAL

Building method

INGREDIENTS

Crème de Cassis (Cassis liqueur)
¾ oz (2.5 cl)
Champagne or a good brut
sparkling wine 4 oz (12 cl)

PREPARATION

Measure ¾ oz (2.5 cl) of Crème de
Cassis in a jigger and pour into a
glass or a wine glass (pre-chilled in the
freezer). Fill almost to the brim with 4 oz
(12 cl) of well-chilled Champagne or brut
sparkling wine. Stir gently with a long-
handled spoon and serve.

SUGGESTED USE

This elegant aperitif is also ideal to enjoy
at all hours of the day

LADY HUGO

Building method

INGREDIENTS

elderflower syrup 1 oz (3 cl)
rosé brut sparkling wine or rosé Champagne 2 oz
(6 cl)
sparkling water or soda water
2 oz (6 cl)

PREPARATION

Measure 1 oz (3 cl) of elderflower syrup in
a jigger and pour into a wine glass filled
with ice. Repeat with 2 oz (6 cl) of rosé brut
sparkling wine or rosé Champagne and 2 oz
(6 cl) of sparkling water or soda water. Stir for
a few seconds and serve, garnished with
1 sprig of mint, ½ a wedge of lemon,
and some edible rose leaves.

SUGGESTED USE

This drink is especially appreciated by
female drinkers.

ALCOHOL CONTENT: 7.4
CALORIES: 152

LAY-OFF

Shake and Strain method

INGREDIENTS

gin 1 oz (3 cl)
white vermouth ¾ oz (2.5 cl)
bitter (Bitter Campari is
recommended) ½ oz (1.5 cl)
orange juice 1 oz (3 cl)

PREPARATION

Measure 1 oz (3 cl) of gin in a
jigger and pour into a shaker.
Repeat with 1 oz (3 cl) of orange
juice, ¾ oz (2.5 cl) of white
vermouth, and ½ oz (1.5 cl) of bitter.
Add a few ice cubes and shake
vigorously for a few seconds. Strain
the drink in a cocktail glass (pre-chilled
in the freezer), holding the ice back
with the strainer, and garnish with a
cocktail cherry and an orange slice.

SUGGESTED USE

Perfect as an aperitif, but it can be
enjoyed at all hours of the day.

LITTLE DAVE

Shake and Strain method

ALCOHOL CONTENT: 8.3

CALORIES: 98

INGREDIENTS

dry white Madeira
1 oz (3 cl)
Aperol ¾ oz (2.5 cl)
bitter (Campari bitter is
recommended) ½ oz (1.5 cl)
orange juice 3 oz (9 cl)

PREPARATION

Measure 1 oz (3 cl) of dry white
Madeira in a jigger and pour
into a shaker. Repeat with ¾ oz
(2.5 cl) of Aperol, ½ oz (1.5 cl)
of bitter and 3 oz (9 cl) of orange
juice. Add a few ice cubes and
shake vigorously for a few seconds.
Holding the ice back with a strainer,
strain the drink into a tall tumbler
filled with ice and serve garnished
with 1 wedge of grapefruit, 1 wedge
of lemon, 1 wedge of orange, and 2
cocktail cherries.

SUGGESTED USE

A sensational aperitif to enjoy at all
hours of the day.

LORY

Shake and Strain method

INGREDIENTS

Aperol 2 oz (6 cl)
bitter (Campari bitter is
recommended) ½ oz (1.5 cl)
peach liqueur 1 oz (3 cl)
orange bitter 3 oz (9 cl)

PREPARATION

Measure 2 oz (6 cl) of Aperol in a
jigger and pour into a shaker. Repeat
with 1 oz (3 cl) of peach liqueur
and ½ oz (1.5 cl) of bitter. Shake
vigorously for a few seconds then,
holding the ice back with a strainer,
strain the drink into a tall tumbler filled
with ice. Fill almost to the brim with 3
oz (9 cl) of orange bitter and mix gently.
Serve, garnished with 1 orange wedge,
1 wedge of grapefruit, 2 cocktail cherries,
and 2 long straws.

SUGGESTED USE

Perfect as an aperitif.

ALCOHOL CONTENT: 13.6
CALORIES: 104

MADEIRA MARTINI

Stir and Strain method

INGREDIENTS

dry vodka 2 oz (6 cl)
dry white Madeira 1 oz (3 cl)

PREPARATION

Measure all the ingredients in a jigger and
pour them into a mixing glass. Add plenty of
ice cubes. Stir with a long-handled spoon,
then, holding the ice back with a strainer,
strain the drink into a cocktail glass pre-
chilled in the freezer. Serve garnished with
some lemon peel and a skewer with 1–2
green olives (be sure to rinse them under
running water to remove the brine).

SUGGESTED USE

An excellent alternative to the Martini
cocktail for happy hour.

ALCOHOL CONTENT: 22.8
CALORIES: 178

MANHATTAN

Stir and Strain method

This Oscar-winning 1959 en travesti comedy directed by Billy Wilder tells about the misadventures of Joe and Jerry (Tony Curtis and Jack Lemmon), two musicians on the run from the underworld. Sugar (Marilyn Monroe), a beautiful, brokenhearted ukulele player, complicates things further. She is so fond of the Manhattan that she even prepares it on a train in a hot water bottle.

INGREDIENTS

Rye, Canadian, or American whiskey
2 oz (6 cl)
red vermouth 1 oz (3 cl)
angostura 1 dash (2–3 drops)

PREPARATION

Measure 2 oz (6 cl) of whiskey in a jigger and pour into a mixing glass. Repeat with 1 oz (3 cl) of red vermouth. Add a dash of angostura (2–3 drops) and some ice cubes. Mix everything together with a long-handled spoon. Strain the drink into a glass (previously chilled in the freezer), holding the ice back with the strainer. Serve, garnished with 2 cocktail cherries.

SUGGESTED USE

One of the most appreciated aperitifs, this drink is also very good for the entire evening.

MARGARITA

Shake and Strain method

ALCOHOL CONTENT: 18.6
CALORIES: 160

In this 2015 blockbuster movie produced by Marvel Studios, a group of superheroes join forces to protect Earth from impending catastrophes. In a famous, funny scene, Tony Stark, or Iron Man (Robert Downey Jr.), tries to convince Bruce Banner, the Hulk (Mark Ruffalo), to work on artificial intelligence instead of sipping Margaritas while sunbathing.

AVENGERS - AGE OF ULTRON

INGREDIENTS

tequila 1½ oz (4.5 cl)
Cointreau or triple sec 1 oz (3 cl)
lemon or lime juice ¾ oz (2.5 cl)
fine salt

PREPARATION

Take a sombrero glass previously chilled in the freezer and moisten half of its rim with some lemon or lime. Dip the glass into a small bowl filled with fine salt so as to coat the damp rim with it. Measure 1½ oz (4.5 cl) of tequila in a jigger and pour into a shaker. Do the same with 1 oz (3 cl) of Cointreau or triple sec and ¾ oz (2.5 cl) of lemon or lime juice. Add ice cubes and shake vigorously for a few seconds. Strain the drink into the sombrero glass, holding the ice back with the strainer, and serve.

SUGGESTED USE

Excellent at all hours of the day.

ALCOHOL CONTENT: 27.2
CALORIES: 203

MARTINI COCKTAIL

Stir and Strain method

ALL ABOUT EVE

Receiving a record number of Oscar nominations, All About Eve is a merciless 1950 portrait of show business, which turned Bette Davis, playing the larger-than-life actress Margo Channing, into a legend. In the movie, there are several interior scenes where drinks become protagonists, and Margo usually sips a Martini Cocktail, a drink that would become one of the most iconic movie drinks of all time.

INGREDIENTS

gin 2½ oz (7.5 cl)
dry vermouth ½ oz (1.5 cl)

PREPARATION

Measure 2½ oz (7.5 cl) of gin in a jigger and pour into a mixing glass. Repeat with ½ oz (1.5 cl) of dry vermouth and add several ice cubes. Stir with a long-handled spoon and strain into a cocktail glass (previously chilled in the freezer), holding the ice back with the strainer. Serve, garnished with 1–2 rinsed green olives skewered on a long toothpick and a lemon rind.

SUGGESTED USE

Dry and slightly aromatic, this drink is the king of aperitifs.

MICHELLE FOREVER

Shake and Strain method

ALCOHOL CONTENT: 8.4
CALORIES: 97

INGREDIENTS
Aperol 1 oz (3 cl)
white vermouth ¾ oz (2.5 cl)
bitter (Campari bitter is
recommended) ½ oz (1.5 cl)
orange juice 3 oz (9 cl)

PREPARATION
Measure 1 oz (3 cl) of Aperol in
a jigger and pour into a shaker.
Repeat with ¾ oz (2.5 cl) of
white vermouth, ½ oz (1.5 cl) of
bitter and 3 oz (9 cl) of orange
juice. Shake vigorously for a few
seconds then, holding the ice back
with a strainer, strain the drink into
a tall tumbler filled with ice. Serve,
garnished with ½ an orange wedge,
½ a lemon wedge, 1 cocktail cherry,
and 2 long straws.

SUGGESTED USE
An excellent aperitif to enjoy throughout
the day.

ALCOHOL CONTENT: 13

CALORIES: 198

MICHELLE ICE

Blending method

INGREDIENTS

Aperol 2 oz (6 cl)
bitter (Campari bitter is
recommended) ½ oz (1.5 cl)
peach vodka 1 oz (3 cl)
ACE (orange/carrot/lemon)
ice cream 5¼ oz (100 g) approx.

PREPARATION

Measure 2 oz (6 cl) of Aperol in a
jigger and pour into a blender. Repeat
with 1 oz (3 cl) of peach vodka and
½ oz (1.5 cl) of bitter. Add 5¼ oz
(100 g) approximately of ACE ice
cream and ½ a low tumbler of crushed
ice. Blend for 15–20 seconds and pour
into a tall tumbler. To serve, garnish with
½ an orange slice and 2 long straws.

SUGGESTED USE

An excellent refreshing aperitif, ideal for
any time of the day.

MIMOSA

Building method

INGREDIENTS

freshly squeezed orange juice
1½ oz (4.5 cl)
brut sparkling wine or Champagne
4 oz (12 cl)

PREPARATION

Measure 1½ oz (4.5 cl) of freshly
squeezed orange juice in a jigger
and pour into a glass or a wine
glass pre-chilled in the freezer. Fill
almost to the brim with 4 oz (12 cl)
of well-chilled brut sparkling wine or
Champagne. Stir gently with a long-
handled spoon and serve, garnished
with 1 orange wedge.

SUGGESTED USE

An excellent aperitif that can be enjoyed
at all hours of the day.

ALCOHOL CONTENT: 14.2
CALORIES: 180

MOJITO "EUROPEAN" TWIST

Muddler method

INGREDIENTS

light or amber rum 1½ oz (4.5 cl)
white or cane sugar 1 tbsp. (20 g) approx.
fresh mint leaves ¼ oz (7 g) approx.
½ lime
soda or sparkling water 2 oz (6 cl)

PREPARATION

Put ½ a lime (cut into cubes) in a tall
tumbler. Add 1 tbsp. (20 g) approximately
of sugar and mash everything with a pestle
until it's pulp. Add ¼ oz (7 g) of mint
leaves, pressing gently against the rest.
Fill the glass with crushed ice or ice cubes
and add 1½ oz (4.5 cl) of light or amber
rum (previously measured in a jigger). Fill to
the rim with 2 oz (6 cl) of soda or sparkling
water and stir for a few seconds with a
long-handled spoon, so as to best mix the
ingredients. To serve, garnish the drink with
2 straws and a nice long sprig of fresh mint.

SUGGESTED USE

To be enjoyed at all hours of the day. Very
suitable as an aperitif.

NEGRONI

Building method

INGREDIENTS

gin 1 oz (3 cl)
red vermouth 1 oz (3 cl)
bitter (Campari Bitter is
recommended) 1 oz (3 cl)

PREPARATION

Measure 1 oz (3 cl) of gin in a jigger
and pour into a low tumbler filled with
ice. Repeat, adding 1 oz (3 cl) of red
vermouth and 1 oz (3 cl) of bitter. Mix
for a few seconds with a long-handled
spoon. Garnish with ½ an orange slice
and serve.

SUGGESTED USE

The Negroni is the aperitif par excellence,
but it can also be enjoyed throughout the
evening.

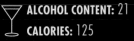

ALCOHOL CONTENT: 21
CALORIES: 125

NEGRONI SBAGLIATO

Building method

INGREDIENTS
bitter (Campari bitter is recommended) 1 oz (3 cl)
red vermouth 1 oz (3 cl)
brut sparkling wine 1 oz (3 cl)

PREPARATION
Measure 1 oz (3 cl) of bitter in a jigger and pour into a low tumbler filled with ice. Repeat with 1 oz (3 cl) of red vermouth. Fill almost to the brim with 1 oz (3 cl) of well-chilled brut sparkling wine and stir gently with a long-handled spoon. To serve, garnish with 1 orange wedge.

SUGGESTED USE
The aperitif par excellence, it is also ideal to enjoy throughout the day and the evening.

NEGROSKY

Building method

INGREDIENTS

dry vodka 1 oz (3 cl)
bitter (Campari Bitter is
recommended) 1 oz (3 cl)
red vermouth 1 oz (3 cl)

PREPARATION

Measure 1 oz (3 cl) of dry vodka in
a jigger and pour into a low tumbler
filled with ice. Repeat with 1 oz (3 cl)
of bitter and 1 oz (3 cl) of red vermouth.
Stir with a long-handled spoon and serve,
garnished with an orange slice.

SUGGESTED USE

It is a valid alternative to the Negroni
cocktail.

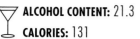
NEW FRED ROSE

Shake and Strain method

INGREDIENTS

gin 1 oz (3 cl)
Mandarinetto Isolabella 1 oz (3 cl)
limoncello ½ oz (1.5 cl)
bitter (Campari Bitter is recommended)
½ oz (1.5 cl)

PREPARATION

Measure 1 oz (3 cl) of gin in a jigger and
pour into a shaker. Repeat with 1 oz (3 cl)
of Mandarinetto Isolabella, ½ oz (1.5 cl)
of bitter, and ½ oz (1.5 cl) of limoncello.
Add some ice cubes and shake vigorously
for a few seconds. Strain the drink into a
cocktail glass (pre-chilled in the freezer),
holding the ice back with the strainer and
serve, garnished with a slice of lemon or
lime and a cocktail cherry.

SUGGESTED USE

A very refreshing drink also recommended
for happy hour.

NEW LULÙ

Shake and Strain method

INGREDIENTS

Aperol 1½ oz (4.5 cl)
bitter (Campari bitter is
recommended) ½ oz (1.5 cl)
peach liqueur ¾ oz (2.5 cl)
orange juice 3 oz (9 cl)

PREPARATION

Measure 1½ oz (4.5 cl) of Aperol in
a jigger and pour in a shaker. Repeat
¾ oz (2.5 cl) of peach liqueur, ½ oz
(1.5 cl) of bitter, and 3 oz (9 cl) of
orange juice. Shake vigorously for a
few seconds, then, holding the ice back
with a strainer, strain the drink into a tall
tumbler filled with ice. Serve, garnished
with ½ a slice of orange, 2 cocktail
cherries, and 2 long straws.

SUGGESTED USE

Excellent as an aperitif, it can be enjoyed
at all hours of the day.

OLD PALE

Stir and Strain method

INGREDIENTS

American whiskey 1 oz (3 cl)
dry vermouth 1 oz (3 cl)
bitter (Campari Bitter is
recommended) 1 oz (3 cl)

PREPARATION

Measure 1 oz (3 cl) of whiskey in a
jigger and pour into a mixing glass.
Repeat with 1 oz (3 cl) of dry vermouth
and 1 oz (3 cl) of bitter. Add a few
ice cubes and stir with a long-handled
spoon. Strain the drink into a glass (pre-
chilled in the freezer), holding the ice
back with the strainer. Serve garnished
with a cocktail cherry.

SUGGESTED USE

A classic aperitif.

OLIVO.0
(OLIVE TREE.O)

by Gianfranco Cacciola

Stir and Strain method

INGREDIENTS

Ulivar (Calabrian olive liqueur)
1¼ oz (4 cl)
gin (Mediterranean) 1¼ oz (4 cl)
extra virgin olive oil 1 dash
(3 drops)

PREPARATION

Measure 1¼ oz (4 cl) of Ulivar in a jigger and
pour into a mixing glass. Repeat with 1¼ oz
(4 cl) of gin and add several ice cubes. Stir
with a long-handled spoon, then, holding the
ice back with a strainer, strain the drink into a
cocktail glass previously chilled in the freezer.
Add 1 dash (3 drops) of extra virgin olive oil
so that it remains on the surface and serve.

SUGGESTED USE

An innovative aperitif, ideal to enjoy at all
hours of the day.

ALCOHOL CONTENT: 22.8
CALORIES: 178

ORIGINAL SPRITZ

Building method

INGREDIENTS

Sauvignon wine 2 oz (6 cl)
sparkling water ½ oz (1.5 cl)

PREPARATION

Measure 2 oz (6 cl) of Sauvignon wine in a jigger and pour it into a wine glass filled with ice. Repeat with ½ oz (1.5 cl) of sparkling water. Stir gently for a few seconds with a long-handled spoon and garnish with ½ a lemon wedge.

SUGGESTED USE

Perfect to enjoy at happy hour. Delicious at all hours.

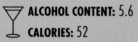 **ALCOHOL CONTENT:** 5.6
CALORIES: 52

PARADISE

Shake and Strain method

INGREDIENTS

gin 1 ½ oz (4.5 cl)
apricot brandy (apricot liqueur) 1 oz (3 cl)
orange juice ¾ oz (2.5 cl)

PREPARATION

Measure 1 ½ oz (4.5 cl) of gin in a jigger and pour into a shaker. Repeat with 1 oz (3 cl) of apricot brandy and ¾ oz (2.5 cl) of orange juice. Add ice cubes and shake vigorously for a few seconds. Strain the drink into a glass (pre-chilled in the freezer), holding the ice back with the strainer, and serve garnished with ½ an orange slice.

SUGGESTED USE

A great drink to enjoy at all hours of the day.

PORT MARTINI

Stir and Strain method

INGREDIENTS
gin 2 oz (6 cl)
White Port 1 oz (3 cl)

PREPARATION
Measure 2 oz (6 cl) gin in a jigger
and pour into a mixing glass. Repeat
with 1 oz (3 cl) of White Port and
add plenty of ice cubes. Stir with a
long-handled spoon, then, holding the
ice back with a strainer, strain the drink
into a cocktail glass pre-chilled in the
freezer. Serve garnished with 3–4 green
olives on a skewer (be sure to rinse them
under running water to remove the brine)
and 1 lemon peel twist.

SUGGESTED USE
A tasty alternative to the Martini cocktail for
happy hour.

ALCOHOL CONTENT: 21.6
CALORIES: 138

PORTOGUESE

Building method

INGREDIENTS
bitter (Campari bitter is recommended)
1 oz (3 cl)
Ruby Port 1 oz (3 cl)
sparkling water or soda water 1 oz (3 cl)

PREPARATION
Measure 1 oz (3 cl) of bitter in a jigger
and pour into a low tumbler filled with
ice. Repeat with 1 oz (3 cl) of Ruby Port.
Fill almost to the brim with 1 oz (3 cl) of
sparkling water or soda water. Stir gently
with a long-handled spoon and serve
garnished with ½ an orange wedge and
some lemon peel.

SUGGESTED USE
A fascinating alternative to the Americano
cocktail for happy hour.

ALCOHOL CONTENT: 5.6
CALORIES: 88

INGREDIENTS

freshly squeezed
tangerine juice 1½ oz
(4.5 cl)
brut sparkling wine or
Champagne 4 oz (12 cl)

PREPARATION

Measure 1½ oz (4.5 cl) of freshly
squeezed tangerine juice in a jigger
and pour into a glass or a wine glass
(pre-chilled in the freezer). Fill almost to
the brim with 4 oz (12 cl) of well-chilled brut
sparkling wine or Champagne. Stir gently with
a long-handled spoon and serve.

SUGGESTED USE

An elegant aperitif that can also be enjoyed throughout
the day.

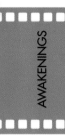

AWAKENINGS

ALCOHOL CONTENT: 21.8
CALORIES: 189

ROB ROY

Stir and Strain method

After having been forgotten for years, the Rob Roy experienced an unexpected worldwide revival thanks to this wonderful 1990 movie based on the life of the multifaceted doctor Oliver Sacks. Robin Williams plays Dr. Malcolm Sayer, a fictional character based on Dr. Sacks. One of his patients awakens from many years of coma and expresses with a shrill tone of voice her desire to drink a Rob Roy.

INGREDIENTS
blended Scotch whisky 2 oz (6 cl)
red vermouth 1 oz (3 cl)
angostura 1 dash (2–3 drops)

PREPARATION
Measure 2 oz (6 cl) of blended Scotch whisky in a jigger and pour into a mixing glass. Repeat with 1 oz (3 cl) of red vermouth. Combine a dash (2–3 drops) of angostura with some ice cubes, then mix it all with a long-handled spoon. Strain the drink into a cocktail glass (pre-chilled in the freezer), holding the ice back with the strainer, and serve garnished with 2 cocktail cherries.

SUGGESTED USE
An excellent aperitif.

ROSSINI
Building method

INGREDIENTS
medium-sized strawberries 5–6
brut sparkling wine or
Champagne 4 oz (12 cl)
strawberry puree (optional)
1 ½ oz (4.5 cl)
still water 1 oz (3 cl)

PREPARATION
Puree 5–6 medium-sized strawberries
with 1 ½ oz (4.5 cl) of strawberry
puree and 1 oz (3 cl) of still water
previously measured in jigger.
Separate 1 oz (3 cl) of the puree and
pour it into a chilled glass (previously
chilled in the freezer). Add 4 oz (12
cl) of well-chilled brut sparkling wine
or Champagne and stir gently with a
long-handle spoon. To serve, garnish
as desired with fresh strawberries.

SUGGESTED USE
To be enjoyed at any hour of the day,
the Rossini is excellent as an aperitif.

ALCOHOL CONTENT: 17.6
CALORIES: 115

SALLY

Building method

INGREDIENTS

dry vodka 1 oz (3 cl)
Aperol 1 oz (3 cl)
bitter (Campari Bitter is
recommended) ½ oz (1.5 cl)
Mandarinetto Isolabella ¾ oz (2.5 cl)

PREPARATION

Measure 1 oz (3 cl) of dry vodka
in a jigger and pour into a low
tumbler filled with ice. Repeat with
1 oz (3 cl) of Aperol, ¾ oz (2.5 cl)
of Mandarinetto Isolabella, and ½ oz
(1.5 cl) of bitter. Stir with a long-handled
spoon and garnish with ½ an orange
slice and 2 cocktail cherries.

SUGGESTED USE

A delicious aperitif that will brighten your
happy hour.

SAMOA

Stir and Strain method

INGREDIENTS

dry vodka 2 oz (6 cl)
peach liqueur ¾ oz (2.5 cl)
bitter (Campari Bitter is recommended)
½ oz (1.5 cl)

PREPARATION

Measure 2 oz (6 cl) of dry vodka in
a jigger and pour into a mixing glass.
Repeat with ½ oz (1.5 cl) of bitter and
¾ oz (2.5 cl) of peach liqueur. Add some
ice cubes and stir with a long-handled
spoon for several seconds. Strain the drink
into a glass (pre-chilled in the freezer),
holding the ice back with the strainer.
To serve, garnish with ½ an orange
slice and a cocktail cherry.

SUGGESTED USE

Excellent as an aperitif and during
celebratory summer nights.

SHERRY MARTINI

Stir and Strain method

INGREDIENTS
dry vodka 2 oz (6 cl)
dry sherry 1 oz (3 cl)

PREPARATION
Measure 2 oz (6 cl) of dry vodka in
a jigger and pour into a mixing glass.
Repeat with 1 oz (3 cl) of dry sherry
and add plenty of ice cubes. Stir with
a long-handled spoon then, holding
the ice back with a strainer, strain the
drink into a cocktail glass pre-chilled in
the freezer. Serve garnished with some
lemon peel and 3–4 green olives on
a skewer (be sure to rinse them under
running water first to remove the brine).

SUGGESTED USE
This drink is an excellent alternative to the
Martini cocktail for happy hour.

 **ALCOHOL CONTENT:** 13.4
CALORIES: 131

SILVIA

Shake and Strain method

INGREDIENTS
Aperol 1 oz (3 cl)
bitter (Campari bitter is
recommended) 1 oz (3 cl)
Müller-Thurgau wine 2 oz (6 cl)
orange juice 2 oz (6 cl)

PREPARATION
Measure 1 oz (3 cl) of Aperol
in a jigger and pour into a shaker.
Repeat with 1 oz (3 cl) of bitter,
2 oz (6 cl) of orange juice, and 2 oz
(6 cl) of Müller-Thurgau. Add a few ice
cubes and shake vigorously for a few
seconds. Holding the ice back with a
strainer, strain the drink into a tall tumbler
filled with ice and serve garnished with
1 slice of lemon and 3 cocktail cherries
tied onto a skewer.

SUGGESTED USE
An excellent aperitif that will brighten the
hottest days.

ALCOHOL CONTENT: 9.8
CALORIES: 122

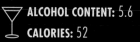

ALCOHOL CONTENT: 5.6
CALORIES: 52

SPRITZ

Building method

INGREDIENTS

brut sparkling wine 2 oz (6 cl)
Aperol 1½ oz (4.5 cl)
sparkling water ½ oz (1.5 cl)

PREPARATION

Measure 1½ oz (4.5 cl) of Aperol in a jigger and pour into a wine glass or a tall tumbler filled with ice. Repeat with 2 oz (6 cl) of brut sparkling wine and ½ oz (1.5 cl) of sparkling water. Stir gently with a long-handled spoon for a few seconds and serve, garnished with ½ an orange slice.

SUGGESTED USE

A must for aperitifs and good at all hours of the day.

SPRITZ CAMPARI
(PIRLO)
Building method

INGREDIENTS
bitter (Campari bitter is recommended) 1½ oz (4.5 cl)
brut sparkling wine 3 oz (9 cl)
sparkling water or soda water 1 oz (3 cl)

PREPARATION
Measure 1½ oz (4.5 cl) of bitter in a jigger and pour into a wine glass filled with ice. Repeat with 3 oz (9 cl) of brut sparkling wine and 1 oz (3 cl) of sparkling water or soda water previously measured in a jigger. Stir gently for a few seconds with a long-handled spoon and serve.

SUGGESTED USE
Among the top drinks for happy hour.

ALCOHOL CONTENT: 8.9
CALORIES: 146

TORRE DI BELEM
(BELEM TOWER)
Building method

INGREDIENTS
Ruby Port 2 oz (6 cl)
bitter (Campari bitter is recommended) 1 oz (3 cl)

PREPARATION
Measure 2 oz (6 cl) of Ruby Port in a jigger and pour into a low tumbler filled with ice. Repeat with 1 oz (3 cl) of bitter. Stir with a long-handled spoon and serve garnished with 2 short straws and ½ a wedge of orange.

SUGGESTED USE
Excellent as an aperitif.

ALCOHOL CONTENT: 11.6
CALORIES: 85

VESCOVO
(BISHOP)

Stir and Strain method

INGREDIENTS
gin 1 ¼ oz (4 cl)
bitter (Campari bitter is
recommended) ½ oz (1.5 cl)
White Port 1 oz (3 cl)

PREPARATION
Measure 1 ¼ oz (4 cl) of gin in a
jigger and pour into a mixing glass.
Repeat with 1 oz (3 cl) of White Port
and ½ oz (1.5 cl) of bitter. Add some
ice cubes and stir gently with a long-
handled spoon for a few seconds.
Holding the ice back with a strainer,
strain the drink into a cocktail glass
pre-chilled in the freezer and serve.

SUGGESTED USE
A refined aperitif for classy events.

ALCOHOL CONTENT: 12.7
CALORIES: 96

VESPER MARTINI TWIST ITALIAN STYLE

Shake and Strain method

INGREDIENTS
gin 2 oz (6 cl)
dry vodka ½ oz (1.5 cl)
white vermouth ½ oz (1.5 cl)
lemon peel (optional)

PREPARATION
Measure 2 oz (6 cl) of gin in a jigger
and pour into a shaker. Repeat with ½ oz
(1.5 cl) of white vermouth and ½ oz
(1.5 cl) of dry vodka. Add some ice cubes
and shake vigorously for a few seconds.
Holding the ice back with a strainer, strain
the drink into a cocktail glass previously
chilled in the freezer and serve.

SUGGESTED USE
Excellent aperitif that pays homage to Agent
007 in *Casino Royale*.

ALCOHOL CONTENT: 25.8

CALORIES: 192

Among the cocktail-movie pairings that have become legendary, the Vesper Martini and 2008's Casino Royale, in which Daniel Craig debuted as James Bond, certainly stand out. Just as in Ian Fleming's 1953 novel of the same name, during a very tense poker game, Agent 007 orders the cocktail, specifying all the ingredients and amounts, thus immediately giving rise to a worldwide fashion.

CASINO ROYALE

VIN CANTO

by Salvatore Bongiovanni

Building method

INGREDIENTS

elderflower syrup ½ oz (1.5 cl)
new red wine 2 oz (6 cl)
gin (preferably rich in botanical
elements) 1 oz (3 cl)

PREPARATION

Measure ½ oz (1.5 cl) of elderflower
syrup in a jigger and pour into a wine
glass filled with ice. Repeat with 1 oz
(3 cl) of gin and 2 oz (6 cl) of new red
wine. Stir gently for a few seconds and
serve garnished with a few blueberries,
red currants, blackberries, and 1 sprig of
mint.

SUGGESTED USE

A delicate digestive drink. Good to enjoy
throughout the evening.

ALCOHOL CONTENT: 8.6
CALORIES: 164

VODKA MARTINI BOND

Shake and Strain method

INGREDIENTS

dry vodka 2½ oz (7.5 cl)
dry vermouth ½ oz (1.5 cl)

PREPARATION

Measure 2½ oz (7.5 cl) of dry vodka
in a jigger and pour into a shaker.
Repeat with ½ oz (1.5 cl) of dry
vermouth. Add a few ice cubes and
shake vigorously for a few seconds.
Strain the drink into a pre-chilled
cocktail glass, holding the ice back
with the strainer and serve, garnished
with a lemon rind and 2–3 green olives,
skewered on a long toothpick.

SUGGESTED USE

One of the most beloved aperitifs, made
popular by the Agent 007 James Bond film
series.

ALCOHOL CONTENT: 24.6
CALORIES: 196

In 1964, the third installment of the James Bond series was released. In the movie, the secret Agent 007 (Sean Connery) utters the iconic line for the first time: "Martini, shaken not stirred," clearly expressing his preference. This request would appear in following installments of the series, becoming a catchphrase that turned this martini into the most iconic movie drink of all time.

WHITE NEGRONI
Building method

INGREDIENTS
gin 1 oz (3 cl)
white vermouth 1 oz (3 cl)
Biancosarti liqueur 1 oz (3 cl)

PREPARATION
Measure 1 oz (3 cl) of gin in a jigger
and pour into a low tumbler filled with ice.
Repeat with 1 oz (3 cl) of white vermouth
and 1 oz (3 cl) of Biancosarti liqueur. Stir
for a few seconds with a long-handled
spoon and serve, garnished with 1 lemon or
lime wedge.

SUGGESTED USE
An intriguing and modern aperitif especially
beloved by female drinkers.

WHITE NEGROSKY

Building method

INGREDIENTS

dry vodka 1 oz (3 cl)
white vermouth 1 oz (3 cl)
Biancosarti liqueur 1 oz (3 cl)

PREPARATION

Measure 1 oz (3 cl) of dry vodka in a jigger and pour into a low tumbler filled with ice. Repeat with 1 oz (3 cl) of white vermouth and 1 oz (3 cl) of Biancosarti liqueur. Stir for a few seconds with a long-handled spoon and serve garnished with 1 lemon or lime wedge.

SUGGESTED USE

An intriguing and modern aperitif especially beloved by female drinkers.

ALCOHOL CONTENT: 15.8
CALORIES: 118

WINE BITTER

Shake and Strain method

INGREDIENTS

Aperol 1 oz (3 cl)
Müller-Thurgau wine 1 oz (3 cl)
peach vodka 1 oz (3 cl)
Sanbittèr 3½ oz (10 cl)

PREPARAZIONE

Measure 1 oz (3 cl) of Aperol in a jigger and pour into a shaker. Repeat with 1 oz (3 cl) of Müller-Thurgau wine and 1 oz (3 cl) of peach vodka. Add a few ice cubes and shake vigorously for a few seconds. Holding the ice back with a strainer, strain the drink into a tall tumbler filled with ice. Add 3½ oz (10 cl) of Sanbittèr, stir, and serve garnished with 2 long straws, ½ a slice of pineapple, and 2 cocktail cherries.

SUGGESTED USE

A great aperitif, ideal to enjoy during the hottest times of the day.

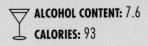

ALCOHOL CONTENT: 7.6
CALORIES: 93

AFTER DINNER
COCKTAILS

This category of great drinks is widespread in the United States, and it has recently started being appreciated throughout Europe as well. It is mainly characterized by its digestive properties, which, in some cases, might even relieve the unpleasant and sometimes painful effects caused by indigestion.

The art of healing stomach pains is ancient. However, not until the first half of the 19th century did small factories start proposing recipes of digestifs to the general public. Bartenders at that time discovered that by mixing some liqueurs with neutral spirits, they could obtain excellent results in the creation of essentially digestive and soothing drinks. Thus, they shaped the precursors of the most modern After Dinner drinks.

One of the most basic methods to create a drink that can facilitate the digestive process is certainly to combine a neutral spirit (e.g., vodka, rum, cognac, brandy) with a sweet liqueur or a cream liqueur (e.g., coffee liqueur, crème de menthe, Amaretto Disaronno). As a matter of fact, sugar stimulates the production of gastric juices, thus significantly improving the well-being of our digestive system. Very popular drinks like the Godmother, the Rusty Nail, or the Black Russian are perfect examples. Another possible way is to combine a spirit with simple syrup and some lemon or lime juice, preferably fresh. This simple combination is found in well-known cocktails like, for example, the Whiskey Sour, the Daiquiri, or the Bacardi Cocktail.

After Dinner drinks are also excellent as desserts after a very good dinner if they include, among their ingredients, one or more sweet liqueurs and ice cream in a range of flavors, including citrus. Another good option is to mix different digestive bitter liqueurs, and the Veterinarian Mojito provides a greatly successful example.

Nowadays, After Dinner drinks have become protagonists of those get-togethers that follow happy hour, whether they end the evening or stretch into the early hours of the day, whether you stay at the same bar or move to another one.

AFTER DINNER COCKTAILS

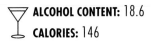
ALBA ALPINA

Shake and Strain method

INGREDIENTS

white grappa   1½ oz (4.5 cl)
white mint liqueur   1 oz (3 cl)
lemon or lime juice   ½ oz (1.5 cl)

PREPARATION

Measure 1½ oz (4.5 cl) of grappa in a jigger and pour into a shaker. Repeat with 1 oz (3 cl) of white mint liqueur and ½ oz (1.5 cl) of lemon or lime juice. Add a few ice cubes and shake vigorously for a few seconds. Strain the drink into a glass (pre-chilled in the freezer) holding the ice back with the strainer, and serve garnished with 4–5 cloves.

SUGGESTED USE

An excellent digestive cocktail.

ALEXANDER

Shake and Strain method

ALCOHOL CONTENT: 13.4
CALORIES: 285

INGREDIENTS

cognac or brandy 1 oz (3 cl)
white chocolate cream 1 oz (3 cl)
cream 1 oz (3 cl)
nutmeg

PREPARATION

Measure 1 oz (3 cl) of brandy or
cognac in a jigger and pour into a
shaker. Repeat with 1 oz (3 cl) of
white chocolate cream and 1 oz (3 cl)
of cream. Add ice cubes and shake
vigorously for a few seconds. Strain
the drink into a glass (pre-chilled in the
freezer), holding the ice back with the
strainer, and garnish with a light dusting
of nutmeg.

SUGGESTED USE

A delicious drink to enjoy throughout the
evening.

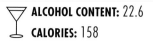

APOTHEKE

Stir and Strain method

INGREDIENTS

cognac or brandy 1 oz (3 cl)
Fernet Branca 1 oz (3 cl)
crème de menthe verte (green mint)
1 oz (3 cl)

PREPARATION

Measure 1 oz (3 cl) of cognac or
brandy in a jigger and pour in a shaker.
Repeat with 1 oz (3 cl) of Fernet Branca
and 1 oz (3 cl) of crème de menthe
verte. Add some ice cubes and stir
vigorously for a few seconds. Strain
the drink into a glass (pre-chilled in the
freezer), holding the ice back with the
strainer, and serve.

SUGGESTED USE

An excellent digestive cocktail, it
is especially recommended for the
evenings.

B-52

Building method

ALCOHOL CONTENT: 11.4
CALORIES: 135

INGREDIENTS

coffee liqueur ¾ oz (2.5 cl)
Baileys ¾ oz (2.5 cl)
Cointreau or Grand Marnier ¾ oz (2.5 cl)

PREPARATION

Measure ¾ oz (2.5 cl) of coffee
liqueur in a jigger and pour into a shot
glass. Measure out ¾ oz (2.5 cl) of
Baileys and ¾ oz (2.5 cl) of Cointreau
or Grand Marnier and layer the
ingredients, in order, into a shot glass
(use a long-handled spoon to slide each
ingredient, separately and gently, into
the shot glass).

SUGGESTED USE

Good as a digestif after a meal.

ALCOHOL CONTENT: 14.6
CALORIES: 128

BACARDI
Shake and Strain method

A MURDER OF CROWS

In a scene from this 1998 thriller, the protagonist, Lawson Russell (Cuba Gooding Jr.), orders a Bacardi Cocktail in a New Orleans bar. He is a young lawyer in crisis, haunted by a mysterious manuscript containing the story of a series of actual murders, which are still unsolved. However, the clues will all point to Russell himself as the prime suspect.

INGREDIENTS

Bacardi light rum 1½ oz (4.5 cl)
lemon or lime juice 1 oz (3 cl)
grenadine syrup ½ oz (1.5 cl)

PREPARATION

Measure 1½ oz (4.5 cl) of Bacardi light rum in a jigger and pour into a shaker. Repeat with 1 oz (3 cl) of lemon or lime juice and ½ oz (1.5 cl) of grenadine syrup. Add some ice cubes and shake vigorously for a few seconds. Strain the drink into a glass (pre-chilled in the freezer), holding the ice back with the strainer, and serve.

SUGGESTED USE

An exquisite digestif that can be enjoyed throughout the day.

BANANA BLISS

Building method

ALCOHOL CONTENT: 21.8
CALORIES: 61

INGREDIENTS

cognac or brandy 1½ oz (4.5 cl)
banana cream 1½ oz (4.5 cl)

PREPARATION

Measure 1½ oz (4.5 cl) of cognac
or brandy in a jigger and pour into a
low tumbler filled with ice. Repeat with
1½ oz (4.5 cl) of banana cream. Stir
with a long-handled spoon and serve.

SUGGESTED USE

A nice digestive drink.

BETWEEN
THE SHEETS

Shake and Strain method

INGREDIENTS

brandy or cognac 1 oz (3 cl)
light rum 1 oz (3 cl)
Cointreau or triple sec 1 oz (3 cl)
lemon or lime juice ½ oz (1.5 cl)

PREPARATION

Measure 1 oz (3 cl) of cognac or
brandy in a jigger and pour into a
shaker. Repeat with 1 oz (3 cl) of light
rum and 1 oz (3 cl) of Cointreau or
triple sec. Add ½ oz (1.5 cl) of lemon
or lime juice (previously measured in a
jigger) and some ice cubes, then shake
vigorously for a few seconds. Strain
the drink into a glass (pre-chilled in the
freezer), holding the ice back with the
strainer, and serve.

SUGGESTED USE

A fantastic drink for the afternoon and
evening. It is also recommended for "spicy"
occasions.

BG 1938

by Demis Vescovi
Building method

INGREDIENTS

red wine (a Bordeaux blend such as Valcalepio
Rosso DOC) ¾ oz (2.5 cl)
bourbon whiskey 1½ oz (4.5 cl)
fresh lime juice ¼ oz (1 cl)
confectioner's sugar 1 tsp. (7 g) approx.
fresh mint ¼ oz (7 g) approx.

PREPARATION

Measure ¼ oz (1 cl) of fresh lime juice in a
jigger and pour into a low tumbler. Add 1
tsp. (7 g) approximately of confectioner's
sugar and 1½ oz (4.5 cl) of bourbon
whiskey. Stir with a long-handled spoon
to dissolve the sugar. Add ¼ oz (7 g)
approximately of fresh mint previously
rubbed with your hands. Add plenty of
flaky or crushed ice and stir again with
a long-handled spoon. Top up with ¾
oz (2.5 cl) of red wine. Garnish with
some mint sprigs and a sprinkling of
confectioner's sugar and serve with
some straws.

SUGGESTED USE

Excellent as an aperitif.

 **ALCOHOL CONTENT:** 17.3
CALORIES: 232

BLACK EGG

Shake and Strain method

INGREDIENTS

tequila 1 oz (3 cl)
coffee liqueur ¾ oz (2.5 cl)
egg yolk ¾ oz (2.5 cl) approx.
cream ¾ oz (2.5 cl)

PREPARATION

Measure 1 oz (3 cl) of tequila in a
jigger and pour into a shaker. Repeat
with ¾ oz (2.5 cl) of coffee liqueur
and ¾ oz (2.5 cl) of cream. Combine
¾ oz (2.5 cl) approximately of egg
yolk, previously measured in a jigger,
and some ice cubes. Shake for a few
seconds, then strain the drink into a
glass (pre-chilled in the freezer), holding
the ice back with the strainer. Serve
garnished with coffee beans.

SUGGESTED USE

An excellent energy-boosting drink,
it is recommended for particularly
challenging days.

BLACK FLY

Shake and Strain method

ALCOHOL CONTENT: 21.8
CALORIES: 214

INGREDIENTS

brandy or cognac 1½ oz (4.5 cl)
coffee liqueur ¾ oz (2.5 cl)
apricot liqueur 1 oz (3 cl)

PREPARATION

Measure 1½ oz (4.5 cl) of brandy or
cognac in a jigger and pour into a
shaker. Repeat with ¾ oz (2.5 cl) of
coffee liqueur and 1 oz (3 cl) of apricot
liqueur. Add a few ice cubes and stir for
a few seconds. Strain the drink into a
glass (pre-chilled in the freezer), holding
the ice back with the strainer, and serve.

SUGGESTED USE

An excellent digestif, it can be enjoyed
at every moment of the day.

48 HRS.

This highly successful 1982 action movie turned former Saturday Night Live *comedian Eddie Murphy into a household name. This buddy-cop, action comedy quickly made the Black Russian, which appears in one of the scenes, into one of the most popular cocktails among young drinkers in bars all over the world.*

BLACK RUSSIAN

Building method

INGREDIENTS

dry vodka 2 oz (6 cl)
coffee liqueur 1 ¼ oz (4 cl)

PREPARATION

Measure 2 oz (6 cl) of dry vodka in a jigger and pour into a low tumbler filled with ice. Repeat with 1 ¼ oz (4 cl) of coffee liqueur. Mix with a long-handled spoon and serve garnished with 2 short straws.

SUGGESTED USE

A drink with excellent digestive properties.

BLACK WINE

Building method

INGREDIENTS

Moscato wine 1 ½ oz (4.5 cl)
coffee liqueur 1 ½ oz (4.5 cl)

PREPARATION

Measure 1 ½ oz (4.5 cl) of Moscato wine in a jigger and pour into a low tumbler filled with ice. Repeat with 1 ½ oz (4.5 cl) of coffee liqueur. Stir with a long-handled spoon and serve garnished with 2 short straws and a few coffee beans.

SUGGESTED USE

An excellent digestif after lunch or dinner.

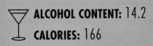 **ALCOHOL CONTENT:** 14.2
CALORIES: 166

BLUE ANGEL

Shake and Strain method

INGREDIENTS

gin 1 oz (3 cl)
Cointreau or triple sec ¾ oz (2.5 cl)
Blue Curaçao ¾ oz (2.5 cl)
lemon or lime juice ½ oz (1.5 cl)

PREPARATION

Measure 1 oz (3 cl) of gin in a jigger
and pour in a shaker. Repeat with ¾ oz
(2.5 cl) of Cointreau or triple sec, ¾ oz
(2.5 cl) of Blue Curaçao, and ½ oz
(1.5 cl) of lemon or lime juice.
Add some ice cubes and shake
vigorously for a few seconds. Strain the
drink into a cocktail glass (previously
chilled in the freezer), holding the ice
back with the strainer, and serve.

SUGGESTED USE

A delicious digestif, perfect to enjoy in
the afternoon or the evening.

BLUE WINE

Shake and Strain method

ALCOHOL CONTENT: 7.7

CALORIES: 112

INGREDIENTS

White Port 1 oz (3 cl)
Cointreau or triple sec
¾ oz (2.5 cl)
Blue Curaçao ½ oz (1.5 cl)
lemon or lime juice ½ oz (1.5 cl)

PREPARATION

Measure 1 oz (3 cl) of White Port in a jigger
and pour into a shaker. Repeat with ¾ oz
(2.5 cl) of Cointreau or triple sec, ½ oz (1.5 cl)
of Blue Curaçao, and ½ oz (1.5 cl) of lemon
or lime juice. Add a few ice cubes and shake
vigorously for a few seconds. Holding the
ice back with a strainer, strain the drink into
a cocktail glass pre-chilled in the freezer and
serve garnished with a skewer of white grapes
and some lemon peel twists.

SUGGESTED USE

Excellent as a digestif, but also to enjoy at all
hours.

BRACCO

Building method

INGREDIENTS
Brachetto wine 2 oz (6 cl)
Aperol 3 oz (9 cl)

PREPARATION
Measure 2 oz (6 cl) of Brachetto
wine in a jigger and pour into a
tall tumbler filled with ice. Repeat
with 3 oz (9 cl) of Aperol. Stir
gently with a long-handled spoon
and serve garnished with 2 long
straws and a few strawberries.

SUGGESTED USE
A delicate aperitif especially
beloved by female drinkers.

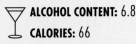
ALCOHOL CONTENT: 6.8
CALORIES: 66

CAIPI SWEET VERMOUTH

Muddler method

INGREDIENTS
½ lime
white or cane sugar 1 tbsp. (20 g)
approx.
white vermouth 2 oz (6 cl)

PREPARATION
Cut ½ a lime into small cubes and put
in a low tumbler together with 1 tbsp.
(20 g) approximately of white or cane
sugar. Grind everything with a pestle
until it is pulp. Fill the glass with crushed
ice or ice cubes and add 2 oz (6 cl) of
white vermouth previously measured in
a jigger. Stir for a few seconds with a
long-handled spoon so as to best mix the
ingredients. Serve garnished with 2 short
straws.

SUGGESTED USE
An excellent aperitif, enjoyable throughout the
day.

ALCOHOL CONTENT: 16.6
CALORIES: 214

CAIPIGRAPPA

Muddler method

INGREDIENTS

white grappa 2 oz (6 cl)
½ lime
white or cane sugar 1 tbsp.
(20 g) approx.

PREPARATION

Put ½ a lime, cut into cubes, in a low tumbler and add 1 tbsp. (20 g) approximately of white or cane sugar. Grind everything with a pestle until it is pulp. Fill the tumbler with crushed ice and add 2 oz (6 cl) of white grappa (previously measured in a jigger). Mix thoroughly with a long-handled spoon and serve, garnished with 2 short straws.

SUGGESTED USE

This excellent digestive drink is perfect to enjoy throughout the evening.

CAIPIRITA

Muddler method

ALCOHOL CONTENT: 16.6
CALORIES: 208

INGREDIENTS

light tequila 2 oz (6 cl)
white or cane sugar
1 tbsp. (20 g) approx.
½ lime

PREPARATION

Place ½ a lime, cut into small
cubes, in a low tumbler and add
1 tbsp. (20 g) approximately of
sugar. With a pestle, pound until it's
pulp. Add 2 oz (6 cl) of light tequila
previously measured in the jigger and
fill almost to the brim with crushed
ice. Stir vigorously for a few seconds
with a long-handled spoon and serve
garnished with 2 short straws.

SUGGESTED USE

A great refreshing drink that combines
perfectly with Mexican cuisine.

CAIPIRITA ANEJO

Muddler method

INGREDIENTS

aged tequila 2 oz (6 cl)
white or cane sugar 1 tbsp.
(20 g) approx.
fresh ½ lime or ¼ orange

PREPARATION

Place ½ a lime or ¼ orange, cut into
small cubes, in a low tumbler and
add 1 tbsp. (20 g) approximately of
white or cane sugar. Grind everything
with a pestle until it is pulp. Add 2
oz (6 cl) of aged tequila previously
measured in a jigger and fill almost to
the brim with crushed ice. Stir vigorously
for a few seconds with a long-handled
spoon and serve, garnished with 2 short
straws.

SUGGESTED USE

Ideal to enjoy at any time of the evening.

CARUSO

Shake and Strain method

INGREDIENTS

gin 1 oz (3 cl)
dry vermouth 1 oz (3 cl)
crème de menthe verte (green mint
liqueur) 1 oz (3 cl)

PREPARATION

Measure 1 oz (3 cl) of gin in a jigger
and pour in a shaker. Repeat with 1 oz
(3 cl) of dry vermouth and 1 oz (3 cl) of
crème de menthe verte. Add a few ice
cubes and shake vigorously for a few
seconds. Strain the drink in a cocktail
glass (previously chilled in the freezer),
holding the ice back with the strainer.

SUGGESTED USE

An extremely enjoyable drink for after
dinner.

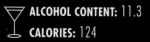

CASANOVA
Muddler method

INGREDIENTS
½ lime
white or cane sugar
1 tbsp. (20 g) approx.
dry vermouth 2 oz (6 cl)
strawberries 3–4

PREPARATION
Cut ½ a lime into small cubes and
put in a low tumbler together with
1 tbsp. (20 g) approximately
of white or cane sugar and 3–4
strawberries. Grind everything with
a pestle until it is pulp. Fill the glass
with crushed ice or ice cubes and add
2 oz (6 cl) of dry vermouth previously
measured in a jigger. Stir for a few
seconds with a long-handled spoon,
so as to best mix the ingredients. Serve
garnished with 2 short straws and 1
strawberry.

SUGGESTED USE
An excellent aperitif, enjoyable
throughout the day.

DAIQUIRI

Shake and Strain method

One of the protagonists of this 1994 small Australian cinematic masterpiece in support of inclusivity is Bernadette (Terence Stamp). During a cathartic journey—aboard a tour bus named Priscilla—made up of music, choreography, and unexpected encounters, Bernadette orders a Lime Daiquiri in a bar. Up to that time, this cocktail was exclusively made with lemon.

INGREDIENTS

white or amber rum 1½ oz (4.5 cl)
lemon or lime juice 1 oz (3 cl)
simple syrup ½ oz (1.5 cl)

PREPARATION

Measure 1½ oz (4.5 cl) of white or amber rum in a jigger and pour into a shaker. Repeat with 1 oz (3 cl) of lemon or lime juice and ½ oz (1.5 cl) of simple syrup. Add a few ice cubes and shake vigorously for a few seconds. Strain the drink into a glass (pre-chilled in the freezer), holding the ice back with the strainer, and serve.

SUGGESTED USE

An excellent refreshing drink.

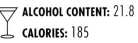**ALCOHOL CONTENT:** 21.8
CALORIES: 185

DAY DREAM

Shake and Strain method

INGREDIENTS

American whiskey 1½ oz (4.5 cl)
crème de menthe verte (green mint)
¾ oz (2.5 cl)
Italian bitter (Rabarbaro Zucca is
recommended) ¾ oz (2.5 cl)

PREPARATION

Measure 1½ oz (4.5 cl) of American
whiskey in a jigger and pour into a
shaker. Repeat with ¾ oz (2.5 cl) of
crème de menthe verte and ¾ oz (2.5
cl) of Rabarbaro Zucca. Add some ice
cubes and shake vigorously for a few
seconds. Holding the ice back with a
strainer, strain the drink into a low tumbler
filled with ice and serve.

SUGGESTED USE

A drink with amazing digestive properties,
it is good for all hours of the evening.

FRENCH CONNECTION

Building method

INGREDIENTS

cognac or brandy 1½ oz (4.5 cl)
Amaretto Disaronno 1½ oz (4.5 cl)

PREPARATION

Measure 1½ oz (4.5 cl) of cognac or brandy in a jigger and pour into a low tumbler filled with ice. Repeat with 1½ oz (4.5 cl) of Amaretto Disaronno. Stir with a long-handled spoon and serve.

SUGGESTED USE

This excellent digestif is suitable for all hours of the evening.

ALCOHOL CONTENT: 23.6
CALORIES: 182

GODFATHER

Building method

THE
GODFATHER

This cocktail is the ultimate expression of how cinema can influence popular culture, including the history of blended drinks. In fact, the Godfather was created in 1972 in the United States to celebrate the release of the movie of the same name, and especially to honor Marlon Brando's memorable performance as Don Vito Corleone.

INGREDIENTS
blended Scotch whisky 1½ oz (4.5 cl)
Amaretto Disaronno 1½ oz (4.5 cl)

PREPARATION
Measure 1½ oz (4.5 cl) of blended Scotch whisky in a jigger and pour into a low tumbler full of ice. Repeat with 1½ oz (4.5 cl) of Amaretto Disaronno. Stir with a long-handled spoon and serve.

SUGGESTED USE
A perfect drink for after dinner.

GODMOTHER

Building method

ALCOHOL CONTENT: 23.4 ▽
CALORIES: 189 🍸

INGREDIENTS

dry vodka 1½ oz (4.5 cl)
Amaretto Disaronno 1½ oz (4.5 cl)

PREPARATION

Measure 1½ oz (4.5 cl) of dry vodka
in a jigger and pour into a low tumbler
filled with ice. Repeat with 1½ oz
(4.5 cl) of Amaretto Disaronno. Stir
with a long-handled spoon and serve.

SUGGESTED USE

An excellent digestif, especially
recommended for the evening.

GRIGIO-VERDE (GREY-GREEN)

Building method

INGREDIENTS

white grappa 2 oz (6 cl)
green mint liqueur 1¼ oz (4 cl)

PREPARATION

Measure 2 oz (6 cl) of white grappa in a jigger and pour into a low tumbler filled with ice. Repeat with 1¼ oz (4 cl) of green mint liqueur. Mix with a long-handled spoon and serve garnished with a nice sprig of fresh mint and 2 short straws.

SUGGESTED USE

A great digestif, it can be enjoyed throughout the evening.

ALCOHOL CONTENT: 21.6
CALORIES: 168

IL SENSO DI ELISA PER IL MESSICO (ELISA'S FEELING FOR MEXICO)

by Silvia Duzioni

Shake and Strain method

INGREDIENTS

light tequila 1½ oz (4.5 cl)
Cointreau or triple sec 1 oz (3 cl)
amaretto syrup ½ oz (1.5 cl)
mint leaves 5–6
orange peel

PREPARATION

Put 5–6 mint leaves in a mixing glass and press them lightly. Measure 1½ oz (4.5 cl) of light tequila in a jigger and pour into the mixing glass. Repeat with 1 oz (3 cl) of Cointreau or triple sec and ½ oz (1.5 cl) of amaretto syrup. Stir for a few seconds with a long-handed spoon and add some ice cubes. Stir again for a bit longer, then, holding the ice back with a double strainer, strain the drink into a cocktail glass previously chilled in the freezer. Spray the top of the drink with the essential oils emanating from the orange peel by pressing it between your fingers, then serve.

SUGGESTED USE

Excellent to enjoy at all hours of the evening. Perfect for after dinner.

ALCOHOL CONTENT: 24.2
CALORIES: 177

ALCOHOL CONTENT: 22.4

CALORIES: 172

LEMON DROP MARTINI

Shake and Strain method

INGREDIENTS

lemon vodka 1 oz (3 cl)
Cointreau or triple sec ¾ oz (2.5 cl)
lemon or lime juice ½ oz (1.5 cl)

PREPARATION

Measure 1 oz (3 cl) of lemon vodka in a jigger and pour into a shaker. Repeat with ¾ oz (2.5 cl) of Cointreau or triple sec and ½ oz (1.5 cl) of lemon or lime juice. Add a few ice cubes and shake vigorously for a few seconds. Holding the ice back with a strainer, strain the drink into a cocktail glass previously chilled in the freezer and serve, garnished with a lemon Chupa Chups lollipop (optional).

SUGGESTED USE

An excellent digestif, perfect to enjoy throughout the evening.

MEDITERRANEAN GIMLET

by Francesco Drago

Shake and Strain method

INGREDIENTS

gin 2 oz (6 cl)
fresh lemon juice 1 oz (3 cl)
ginger syrup ½ oz (1.5 cl)
Sirene Mediterraneo aromatic bitter 1 dash (2 drops)
fresh basil 2–3 leaves
rosemary

PREPARATION

Measure 2 oz (6 cl) of gin in a jigger and pour into a shaker. Repeat with 1 oz (3 cl) of fresh lemon juice and ½ oz (1.5 cl) of ginger syrup. Add 1 dash (2 drops) of bitter, 2–3 basil leaves, and 1 sprig of rosemary, then mix everything with a long-handled spoon so that the herbs release their essential oils. Finally, add some ice cubes and shake vigorously for a few seconds. Holding the ice back with a doble strainer, strain the drink into a low tumbler filled with ice and serve garnished with 1 sprig of rosemary, basil leaves, and lemon peel.

SUGGESTED USE

A great drink to enjoy at all hours.

ALCOHOL CONTENT: 16.7
CALORIES: 179

MEDITERRANEO
(MEDITERRANEAN)
Muddler method

INGREDIENTS
dry Marsala 2 oz (6 cl)
white or cane sugar 1 tbsp. (20 g)
approx.
fresh mint ½ oz (3 g) approx.
fresh basil ½ oz (3 g) approx.
sparkling water or soda water 2 oz (6 cl)
½ lime

PREPARATION
Cut ½ a lime into small cubes and put
in a tall tumbler. Add 1 tbsp. (20 g)
approximately of white or cane sugar
and grind everything with a pestle until it
is pulp. Add ½ oz (3 g) approximately of
mint and ½ oz (3 g) approximately of basil,
gently pressing them. Fill the glass with ice
cubes or crushed ice and add 2 oz (6 cl) of
dry Marsala. Fill almost to the brim with 2 oz
(6 cl) of sparkling water or soda water.
Stir for a few seconds with a long-handled
spoon. Serve garnished with two long straws,
1 sprig of fresh mint, and 1 sprig of basil.

SUGGESTED USE
A great aperitif.

ALCOHOL CONTENT: 6.4
CALORIES: 178

MEZCALIBUR
Shake and Strain method

INGREDIENTS
mezcal 1½ oz (4.5 cl)
spearmint liqueur ¾ oz (2.5 cl)
Maraschino liqueur ½ oz (1.5 cl)
pineapple juice 3 oz (9 cl)

PREPARATION
Measure 1½ oz (4.5 cl) of mezcal in a
jigger and pour into a shaker. Repeat with
¾ oz (2.5 cl) of spearmint liqueur, ½ oz
(1.5 cl) of Maraschino liqueur and 3 oz
(9 cl) of pineapple juice. Add some ice
cubes and shake vigorously for a few
seconds. Holding the ice back with a strainer,
strain the drink into a tall tumbler filled with
ice and serve, garnished with ½ a slice of
pineapple, ½ an orange slice, 1 nice sprig
of fresh mint, and 2 long straws.

SUGGESTED USE
A long drink that is particularly recommended
during the hottest days of summer.

ALCOHOL CONTENT: 17.3
CALORIES: 174

MODÌ
by Filippo Fratton
Building method

INGREDIENTS
Amaretto Disaronno 1¼ oz (3.75 cl)
Moscato d'Asti DOCG wine ¾ oz
(2.5 cl)
orange juice (not blood orange) 3 oz
(9 cl)
grenadine syrup ½ oz (1.5 cl)

PREPARATION
Measure 1¼ oz (3.75 cl) of Amaretto
Disaronno in a jigger and pour into a
tall tumbler filled with ice. Repeat with
¾ oz (2.5 cl) of Moscato d'Asti DOCG
and 3 oz (9 cl) of orange juice (not blood
orange). Stir gently with a long-handled
spoon and add ½ oz (1.5 cl) of grenadine
syrup. Garnish with ½ an orange wedge
and a few cocktail cherries.

SUGGESTED USE
A perfect drink for any time of the day.

ALCOHOL CONTENT: 14
CALORIES: 160

MOJITO DIGESTIVO
(DIGESTIF MOJITO)
Muddler method

INGREDIENTS
white grappa ¾ oz (2.5 cl)
Amaro Braulio ¾ oz (2.5 cl)
Amaro Ramazzotti (or other Italian bitter)
¾ oz (2.5 cl)
½ lime
fresh mint ¼ oz (7 g) approx.
white or cane sugar 1 tbsp. (20 g) approx.
soda water or sparkling water 2 oz (6 cl)

PREPARATION
Put ½ a lime, cut into small cubes, in
a tall tumbler and add 1 tbsp. (20 g)
approximately of white or cane sugar.
Grind everything with a pestle until it is pulp.
Add ¼ oz (7 g) approximately of fresh mint,
gently pressing it down. Fill the tumbler with
crushed ice or ice cubes and add ¾ oz
(2.5 cl) of Amaro Braulio, ¾ oz (2.5 cl) of
white grappa, and ¾ oz (2.5 cl) of Amaro
Ramazzotti (previously measured in a jigger).
Fill almost to the brim with 2 oz (6 cl) of
soda water or sparkling water and mix with
a long-handled spoon, so as to best blend the
ingredients. Serve, garnished with 1 nice sprig
of mint and 2 long straws.

SUGGESTED USE
An excellent digestive drink.

MOJITO VETERINARIO
(VETERINARIAN MOJITO)

Muddler method

INGREDIENTS

Amaro Montenegro 2 oz (6 cl)
½ lime
fresh mint ¼ oz (7 g) approx.
white or cane sugar 1 tbsp. (20 g)
approx.
soda water or sparkling water 2 oz
(6 cl)

PREPARATION

Cut ½ a lime into cubes. Put the lime
cubes in a tall tumbler and add
1 tbsp. (20 g) approximately of white
or cane sugar. Grind everything with
a pestle until it is pulp. Add ¼ oz
(7 g) approximately of fresh mint leaves
and press them lightly. Fill the glass with
crushed ice or ice cubes and add 2 oz
(6 cl) of Amaro Montenegro (previously
measured in a jigger). Fill almost to the
brim with 2 oz (6 cl) of soda water or
sparkling water and mix with a long-
handled spoon so that the ingredients
blend well. To serve, garnish with 1 nice
sprig of fresh mint and 2 long straws.

SUGGESTED USE

An excellent digestif, it is suitable for the
entire evening.

OLD FASHIONED

Building method

ALCOHOL CONTENT: 17.2

CALORIES: 180

One of the protagonists of this pleasant and bittersweet 2011 comedy is Jacob Palmer, played by Ryan Gosling. Jacob, a womanizer, teaches Cal Weaver (Steve Carell) his effective seduction techniques. In the movie, he uses the Old Fashioned as a winning technique to seduce one of his victims, even though things eventually will not go as expected and both he and Cal will be led to reflect on the correct ways to approach and relate to women.

CRAZY, STUPID, LOVE

INGREDIENTS
American whiskey 2 oz (6 cl)
angostura 1 dash (2–3 drops)
still water 1 oz (3 cl)
white sugar 1 lump

PREPARATION
Place 1 lump of white sugar in the center of a low tumbler, moistened with a dash (2–3 drops) of angostura. Measure 1 oz (3 cl) of still water in a jigger and add it to the glass. Fill with some ice and add 2 oz (6 cl) of whiskey (previously measured in a jigger). Stir gently with a long-handled spoon and serve, garnished with a cocktail cherry, ½ a slice of orange, and 2 short straws.

SUGGESTED USE
A great drink to enjoy as an aperitif or throughout the evening.

PINK CHAMPAGNE COCKTAIL

Building method

INGREDIENTS

brandy or cognac ½ oz (1.5 cl)
rosé Champagne or rosé brut
sparkling wine 3 oz (9 cl)
sugar lump 1
Grand Marnier ½ oz (1.5 cl)
angostura 1 dash (2–3 drops)

PREPARATION

Put 1 sugar lump in a glass or wine
glass pre-chilled in the freezer and
moisten it with 1 dash of angostura
(2–3 drops). Add ½ oz (1.5 cl) of
brandy or cognac and ½ oz (1.5
cl) of Grand Marnier previously
measured in a jigger. Repeat with
3 oz (9 cl) of well-chilled rosé
Champagne or rosé brut sparkling
wine. Stir gently with a long-handled
spoon and serve, garnished with ½ a
slice of orange and cocktail cherries.

SUGGESTED USE

Excellent aperitif especially loved by
women.

RUSTY NAIL

Building method

ALCOHOL CONTENT: 26.2
CALORIES: 184

INGREDIENTS

blended Scotch whisky 2 oz (6 cl)
Drambuie liqueur 1 oz (3 cl)

PREPARATION

Measure 2 oz (6 cl) of whisky in a
jigger and pour into a low tumbler
full of ice. Repeat with 1 oz (3 cl)
of Drambuie liqueur. Stir for a few
seconds with a long-handled spoon
and serve.

SUGGESTED USE

An excellent digestif, this drink is
especially recommended at the end of
a big dinner.

SAMOS MARTINI

Shake and Strain method

INGREDIENTS
dry vodka 2 oz (6 cl)
sweet Samos wine 1 oz (3 cl)

PREPARATION
Measure 2 oz (6 cl) of dry vodka
in a jigger and pour into a mixing
glass. Repeat with 1 oz (3 cl) of
sweet Samos wine and add plenty
of ice cubes. Stir with a long-handled
spoon then, holding the ice back with
a strainer, strain the drink into a cocktail
glass pre-chilled in the freezer. Serve
garnished with some lemon peel and
2 grapes on a long skewer.

SUGGESTED USE
An excellent digestif, good to enjoy at all
hours.

 **ALCOHOL CONTENT:** 12.2
CALORIES: 142

SAZERAC TWIST ON THE ROCKS

Shake and Strain method

INGREDIENTS
American whiskey 1 oz (3 cl)
brandy or cognac ¾ oz (2.5 cl)
absinthe ½ oz (1.5 cl)
sugar 1 lump
angostura 1 dash (2–3 drops)

PREPARATION
Measure 1 oz (3 cl) of American
whiskey in a jigger and pour into a
mixing glass. Repeat with ¾ oz (2.5 cl)
of brandy or cognac and ½ oz (1.5 cl)
of absinthe. Add 1 sugar lump moistened
with 1 dash (2–3 drops) of angostura and
some ice. Stir everything with a long-
handled spoon then, holding the ice back
with a strainer, strain the drink into a low
tumbler filled with ice and serve garnished
with some lemon peel.

SUGGESTED USE
An excellent aperitif.

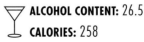 **ALCOHOL CONTENT:** 26.5
CALORIES: 258

This 2008 movie is a wonderful work with a touch of fantasy based on a well-known short story by F. Scott Fitzgerald. It tells in flashback the surprising life of the protagonist, played by Brad Pitt, who was literally born old. It all starts in the early 1920s, when the Sazerac was particularly appreciated, so much so that it is ordered in one of the very first scenes.

THE CURIOUS CASE OF BENJAMIN BUTTON

ALCOHOL CONTENT: 23.5
CALORIES: 280

STINGER ICE

Blending method

INGREDIENTS

brandy 1½ oz (4.5 cl)
crème de menthe blanche (white
mint) 1½ oz (4.5 cl)
lemon ice cream 5¼ oz (100 g)
approx.

PREPARATION

Measure 1½ oz (4.5 cl) of brandy
in a jigger and pour into a blender.
Repeat with 1½ oz (4.5 cl) of crème de
menthe blanche. Add 5¼ oz (100 g)
approximately of lemon ice cream and
½ a low tumbler of crushed ice. Blend
for 15–20 seconds and pour into a tall
tumbler. Serve, garnished with a slice of
lemon, 1 sprig of fresh mint, and 2 long
straws.

SUGGESTED USE

A great digestive and thirst-quenching drink.

FROZEN STRAWBERRY DAIQUIRI

Blending method

ALCOHOL CONTENT: 10.2

CALORIES: 89

INGREDIENTS

light or amber rum 1½ oz (4.5 cl)
lime or lemon juice ¾ oz (2.5 cl)
simple syrup ¾ oz (2.5 cl)
fresh strawberries 3–4
strawberry puree ½ oz (1.5 cl)

PREPARATION

Measure 1½ oz (4.5 cl) of light or
amber rum in a jigger and transfer it to
a blender. Repeat with ¾ oz (2.5 cl) of
simple syrup, ¾ oz (2.5 cl) of lemon or
lime juice, and ½ oz (1.5 cl) of strawberry
puree. Add 1 tall tumbler of crushed ice
and 3–4 fresh strawberries. Blend for
15–20 seconds and pour into the tumbler.
Serve, garnished with strawberries and 2
long straws.

SUGGESTED USE

A very refreshing drink that can be enjoyed at
any time of day.

SWEET AFTER EIGHT

Blending method

INGREDIENTS

white crème de nenthe or mint
liqueur 1 ½ oz (4.5 cl)
chocolate liqueur 1 ½ oz (4.5 cl)
Moscato wine 2 oz (6 cl)

PREPARATION

Measure 1 ½ oz (4.5 cl) of white
crème de menthe or mint liqueur in a
jigger and pour into a blender. Repeat
with 1 ½ oz (4.5 cl) of chocolate
liqueur. Add 2 oz (6 cl) of Moscato
wine and ½ a low tumbler of crushed
ice. Blend for 15–20 seconds and pour
into a tall tumbler. Serve garnished with 2
long straws and 1 sprig of fresh mint.

SUGGESTED USE

An excellent digestif, especially
recommended for the hottest times.

ALCOHOL CONTENT: 13.6
CALORIES: 173

THE BEST

Shake and Strain method

INGREDIENTS

brandy or cognac 1 ½ oz (4.5 cl)
coffee liqueur 1 oz (3 cl)
Cointreau or triple sec ¾ oz (2.5 cl)

PREPARATION

Measure 1 ½ oz (4.5 cl) of brandy
or cognac in a jigger and pour into a
shaker. Repeat with 1 oz (3 cl) of coffee
liqueur and ¾ oz (2.5 cl) of Cointreau or
triple sec. Add a few ice cubes and stir
for a few seconds. Holding the ice back
with a strainer, strain the drink into a low
tumbler filled with ice and serve.

SUGGESTED USE

A perfect drink for after dinner, it is
particularly suitable as a digestif.

TIRAMISÙ ICE

Blending method

INGREDIENTS

coffee liqueur 1 oz (3 cl)
egg liqueur 1 oz (3 cl)
dark rum 1½ oz (4.5 cl)
milk-flavored ice cream or vanilla ice
cream 5¼ oz (100 g) approx.
unsweetened cocoa powder

PREPARATION

Measure 1 oz (3 cl) of egg liqueur in a
jigger and pour into a blender. Repeat
with 1½ oz (4.5 cl) of dark rum and 1
oz (3 cl) of coffee liqueur. Add 5¼ oz
(100 g) approximately of milk-flavored or
vanilla ice cream and ½ a low tumbler of
crushed ice. Blend for 15–20 seconds and
pour into a tall tumbler. Serve, garnished
with a dusting of unsweetened cocoa
powder and 2 long straws.

SUGGESTED USE

A gourmet after-dinner drink, it is also good as
a digestif.

ALCOHOL CONTENT: 19
CALORIES: 380

TONY'S

by Antonello Gagliardi

Shake and Strain method

INGREDIENTS

White Port 1 oz (3 cl)
dry vodka ¾ oz (2.5 cl)
Drambuie 1 oz (3 cl)
whiskey ¼ oz (1 cl)

PREPARATION

Measure 1 oz (3 cl) of White Port in a
jigger and pour into a shaker. Repeat with
¾ oz (2.5 cl) of dry vodka, 1 oz (3 cl) of
Drambuie, and ¼ oz (1 cl) of whiskey.
Add a few ice cubes and shake vigorously
for a few seconds. Holding the ice back
with a strainer, strain the drink into a
cocktail glass pre-chilled in the freezer
and serve garnished with 1 sprig of mint
and some lemon and orange peel twists.

SUGGESTED USE

A great digestive drink. Good to enjoy
throughout the evening.

ALCOHOL CONTENT: 22.6
CALORIES: 218

ALCOHOL CONTENT: 17.2
CALORIES: 126

TWIST HEMINGWAY DAIQUIRI (PAPA DOBLE)

Blending method

INGREDIENTS

light rum 1½ oz (4.5 cl)
grapefruit juice ¾ oz (2.5 cl)
lime or lemon juice ¾ oz (2.5 cl)
Maraschino liqueur ½ oz (1.5 cl)

PREPARATION

Measure 1½ oz (4.5 cl) of light rum in a jigger and pour into a blender. Repeat with ½ oz (1.5 cl) of Maraschino liqueur, ¾ oz (2.5 cl) of lemon or lime juice, and ¾ oz (2.5 cl) of grapefruit juice. Add 3 tablespoons of crushed ice and blend for about 15 seconds. Pour into a low tumbler and serve, garnished with 1 grapefruit segment and 2 short straws.

SUGGESTED USE

An excellent refreshing drink.

WHISKEY SOUR

Shake and Strain method

ALCOHOL CONTENT: 11.8
CALORIES: 120

A good cocktail can often become an ally if you want to seduce someone. This is what happens in this delightful 1955 comedy, where the drink in question is the Whiskey Sour and the aspiring seducer is Richard Sherman (Tom Ewell). When his wife and son leave for the summer holidays, he stays at home by himself due to his job. Literally struck by the beauty of his upstairs neighbor (Marilyn Monroe), Richard dangerously starts daydreaming…

THE SEVEN YEAR ITCH

INGREDIENTS

whiskey 1½ oz (4.5 cl)
lemon or lime juice 1¼ oz (4 cl)
simple syrup ¾ oz (2.5 cl)

PREPARATION

Measure 1½ oz (4.5 cl) of whiskey in a jigger and pour into a shaker. Repeat with 1¼ oz (4 cl) of lemon or lime juice and ¾ oz (2.5 cl) of simple syrup. Add some ice cubes and shake vigorously for a few seconds. Strain the drink into a cocktail glass (pre-chilled in the freezer), holding the ice back with the strainer, and serve garnished with a cocktail cherry (optional).

SUGGESTED USE

An excellent digestif, this drink is great to enjoy throughout the evening.

 **ALCOHOL CONTENT:** 22.5
CALORIES: 160

WHITE LADY

Shake and Strain method

INGREDIENTS

gin 1½ oz (4.5 cl)
Cointreau or triple sec 1 oz (3 cl)
lemon or lime juice ¾ oz (2.5 cl)

PREPARATION

Measure 1½ oz (4.5 cl) of gin in a
jigger and pour into a shaker. Repeat
with 1 oz (3 cl) of Cointreau or triple
sec and ¾ oz (2.5 cl) of lemon or lime
juice. Add some ice cubes and shake
vigorously for a few seconds. Strain the
drink into a cocktail glass (pre-cooled in
the freezer), holding the ice back with the
strainer, and serve.

SUGGESTED USE

A refined cocktail with effective digestive
properties.

WHITE SPIDER

Building method

ALCOHOL CONTENT: 23.2
CALORIES: 289

INGREDIENTS

dry vodka 1½ oz (4.5 cl)
crème de menthe blanche (white mint liqueur) 1½ oz (4.5 cl)

PREPARATION

Measure 1½ oz (4.5 cl) of dry vodka in a jigger and pour into a low tumbler filled with ice. Repeat with 1½ oz (4.5 cl) of crème de menthe blanche. Mix with a long-handled spoon and serve, garnished with a nice sprig of fresh mint and 2 short straws.

SUGGESTED USE

A refreshing drink, it is very effective as a digestif.

WINE & LIQUORICE

Building method

INGREDIENTS
Moscato wine 1 ½ oz (4.5 cl)
licorice liqueur 1 ½ oz (4.5 cl)

PREPARATION
Measure 1 ½ oz (4.5 cl) of Moscato wine in a jigger and pour into a low tumbler filled with ice. Repeat with 1 ½ oz (4.5 cl) of licorice liqueur. Stir with a long-handled spoon and serve garnished with 2 short straws and 2 licorice wheels.

SUGGESTED USE
An excellent digestif.

WINE APPLE MARTINI

Shake and Strain method

INGREDIENTS
Lugana white wine 1½ oz (4.5 cl)
apple liqueur ¾ oz (2.5 cl)
Cointreau or triple sec ¾ oz (2.5 cl)

PREPARATION
Measure 1½ oz (4.5 cl) of Lugana
white wine in a jigger and pour into
a shaker. Repeat with ¾ oz (2.5 cl)
of apple liqueur and ¾ oz (2.5 cl) of
Cointreau or triple sec. Add a few ice
cubes and shake for a few seconds.
Holding the ice back with a strainer,
strain the drink into a cocktail glass pre-
chilled in the freezer, and serve garnished
with a few white grapes.

SUGGESTED USE
Excellent as an aperitif, but also enjoyable
at all hours of the day.

ALCOHOL CONTENT: 13.3
CALORIES: 165

WINE FRENCH KISS

Building method

INGREDIENTS
strawberry puree or smoothie
1 oz (3 cl)
pineapple juice 1 oz (3 cl)
brut sparkling wine or Champagne 3 oz (9 cl)

PREPARATION
Measure 1 oz (3 cl) of strawberry puree
or smoothie in a jigger and pour into
a wine glass. Repeat with 1 oz (3 cl) of
pineapple juice. Stir well with a long-
handled spoon and fill with 3 oz (9
cl) of well-chilled brut sparkling wine
or Champagne. Stir gently for a few
seconds and serve, garnished with
1 strawberry.

SUGGESTED USE
This special variant of the Rossini is
perfect as an aperitif, but it is also
recommended at all hours of the day.

ALCOHOL CONTENT: 10.3
CALORIES: 104

COOL
DRINKS

Cool Drinks have always been considered fashionable.

Beloved by fashion lovers who appreciate their originality and the variety of their alcohol content, these drinks are especially popular among the most demanding and curious young drinkers.

Some Cool Drinks like the Tequila Bum Bum, the Original Cuban Mojito, the Kamikaze, or the Toro Loco have achieved great success and have become worldwide evergreens over the years. Many Cool Drinks were born as innovative interpretations of classic cocktails with the aim of anticipating, understanding, and satisfying the changing taste trends and bar clientele. Particularly remarkable are those cocktails born as interesting alternatives to the classic Mojito: the Mojito Fidel, the Mojito Basito, and the Passion Mojito. These drinks have been met with great support, especially among female drinkers, who are becoming more demanding every day. Among the most recent Cool Drinks are the Moscow Mule, the Spritz Mojito, and the Tommy Margarita, which are increasingly capable of enlivening not only the counters of the most fashionable bars, but also very exclusive private parties.

This family of drinks is often associated with the world of fashion, cinema, TV series, and pop music, and their long-lasting success has turned some of these cocktails into real classics.

One of the most striking examples is the Cosmopolitan. This cocktail was created in Miami by the bartender Cherry Cook on commission for a well-known liqueur company, whose aim was to launch into the market a new drink that could meet the delicate taste of the growing female public. The recipe combines liqueurs, citruses, and cranberry juice, giving rise to a bright pink drink served in a perfectly fitting and elegant Martini glass. The Cosmopolitan reached the peak of its success in the second half of the '90s thanks to Madonna. The photo of her sipping a Cosmopolitan at the Rainbow Room was enough to make it immortal and strengthen its fame as a cocktail beloved by modern, intelligent, and determined women, such as Carrie Bradshaw and her group of friends in *Sex and the City*.

COOL DRINKS

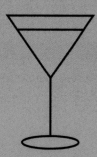

1989

by Giulia Gobbi

Building method

INGREDIENTS

dry vodka ¾ oz (2.5 cl)
Albana di Romagna dei Colli
Romagnoli sweet wine 1½ oz
(4.5 cl)
tonic water ¾ oz (2.5 cl)
juice from ½ a wedge of lime

PREPARATION

Measure ¾ oz (2.5 cl) of dry vodka
in a jigger and pour into a low tumbler
filled with ice. Repeat with 1½ oz (4.5
cl) of Albana di Romagna sweet wine.
Fill almost to the brim with ¾ oz (2.5 cl)
of tonic water and add the juice of ½
a wedge of lime. Stir gently with a long-
handled spoon and serve garnished with
½ a wedge of lime.

SUGGESTED USE

Excellent as an aperitif, but also delicious
to enjoy at any time of the day.

ALCOHOL CONTENT: 14.2
CALORIES: 166

ALESSANDRO MASSIMO 2014

Building method

INGREDIENTS

Müller-Thurgau wine 1½ oz (4.5 cl)
crème de menthe verte (green mint)
1½ oz (4.5 cl)

PREPARATION

Measure 1½ oz (4.5 cl) of Müller-Thurgau
wine in a jigger and pour into a low
tumbler filled with ice. Repeat with 1½ oz
(4.5 cl) of green crème de menthe verte.
Stir with a long-handled spoon and serve
garnished with 2 short straws, 1 sprig of
mint, and a candy pacifier.

SUGGESTED USE

An excellent and refreshing digestif,
recommended for very sultry days.

AFTER EIGHT

Blending method

INGREDIENTS

mint liqueur 1½ oz (4.5 cl)
chocolate liqueur 1½ oz (4.5 cl)
mint ice cream 2¾ oz (50 g)
approx.
chocolate ice cream 2¾ oz (50 g)
approx.

PREPARATION

Measure 1½ oz (4.5 cl) of mint
liqueur in a jigger and pour into
a blender. Repeat with 1½ oz
(4.5 cl) of chocolate liqueur. Add
2¾ oz (50 g) approximately of
mint ice cream, 2¾ oz (50 g)
approximately of chocolate ice cream,
and ½ a low tumbler of crushed ice.
Blend for 15–20 seconds and pour
into a tall tumbler. To serve, garnish
with 1 nice sprig of fresh mint and
2 long straws.

SUGGESTED USE

A gourmet drink that can be enjoyed
throughout the evening. It is also good
as a digestif.

AMARETTO COLADA

Blending method

INGREDIENTS

Amaretto Disaronno 1½ oz (4.5 cl)
pineapple juice 2 oz (6 cl)
light rum ¾ oz (2.5 cl)
coconut puree 1 oz (3 cl)

PREPARATION

Measure ¾ oz (2.5 cl) of light rum in a jigger and transfer to a blender. Repeat with 1½ oz (4.5 cl) of Amaretto Disaronno, 2 oz (6 cl) of pineapple juice, and 1 oz (3 cl) of coconut puree. Add ½ a low tumbler of crushed ice and blend for 15–20 seconds. Pour into a tall tumbler and serve, garnished with ¼ a slice of pineapple, 2 cocktail cherries, and 2 long straws.

SUGGESTED USE

This long drink is particularly suitable for afternoons.

ALCOHOL CONTENT: 18.4
CALORIES: 150

APPLE MARTINI
Shake and Strain method

INGREDIENTS

dry vodka 1½ oz (4.5 cl)
green apple liqueur ¾ oz (2.5 cl)
Cointreau or triple sec ¾ oz (2.5 cl)

PREPARATION

Measure 1½ oz (4.5 cl) of dry vodka in a jigger and pour into a shaker. Repeat with ¾ oz (2.5 cl) of green apple liqueur and ¾ oz (2.5 cl) of Cointreau or triple sec. Add ice cubes and stir for a few seconds. Strain the drink into a glass (pre-chilled in the freezer), holding the ice back with the strainer, and serve.

SUGGESTED USE

A perfect drink for happy hour.

ARNOLD PALMER

Building method

ALCOLOL CONTENT: 0
CALORIES: 92

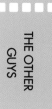

This cop-buddy, action comedy, starring Will Ferrell and Mark Wahlberg, was a surprise 2010 box office hit. In one scene, spiked Arnold Palmers are served to the two unkempt detectives. Thanks in part to the movie, this drink has become such a success over the last decade that you can easily find it in liquor stores.

THE OTHER GUYS

INGREDIENTS
lemon iced tea 3 oz (9 cl)
lemonade 3 oz (9 cl)

PREPARATION
Measure 3 oz (9 cl) of lemon iced tea in a jigger and pour into a tall tumbler filled with ice. Repeat with 3 oz (9 cl) of lemonade. Stir gently with a long-handled spoon and serve, garnished with 1 lemon wedge (optional).

SUGGESTED USE
An excellent non-alcoholic and refreshing drink. There is also an alcoholic version of this drink made with 2 oz (6 cl) of dry vodka, 2 oz (6 cl) of lemon iced tea, and 2 oz (6 cl) of lemonade.

AROMATIC SPRITZ

Building method

INGREDIENTS
Sauvignon wine 3 oz (9 cl)
sparkling water or soda water 2 oz (6 cl)

PREPARATION
Measure 2 oz (6 cl) of sparkling water or soda water in a jigger and pour into a tall tumbler filled with ice. Fill almost to the brim with Sauvignon wine and stir for a few seconds. Serve, garnished with 2 long straws and 1 lemon wedge.

SUGGESTED USE
An excellent aperitif, also recommended to enliven any time of the day.

ALCOHOL CONTENT: 8.8
CALORIES: 156

ABSINTHE MOJITO

Muddler method

INGREDIENTS
absinthe (45% vol.) 2 oz (6 cl)
½ lime
fresh mint ¼ oz (7 g) approx.
white or cane sugar 1 tbsp.
(20 g) approx.
soda water or sparkling water 2 oz (6 cl)

PREPARATION
Cut ½ a lime into cubes and put in a tall tumbler with 1 tbsp. (20 g) approximately of white or cane sugar. Grind everything with a pestle until it is pulp. Add ¼ oz (7 g) approximately of fresh mint and press it lightly against the glass. Fill with crushed ice or ice cubes and add 2 oz (6 cl) of absinthe (previously measured in a jigger). Fill almost to the brim of the tumbler with 2 oz (6 cl) of soda water or sparkling water. Mix everything with a long-handled spoon so that the ingredients blend well. To serve, garnish with 1 sprig of fresh mint and 2 long straws.

SUGGESTED USE
An excellent and fashionable drink.

ALCOHOL CONTENT: 14.2
CALORIES: 172

ALCOHOL CONTENT: 13.6
CALORIES: 132

FROZEN BANANA DAIQUIRI

Blending method

The eagerly awaited second installment of the trilogy about the powerful Corleone crime family, directed by Francis Ford Coppola, came out in 1974. In a scene from this adaptation of the well-known novel by Mario Puzo, which boasted a star-studded cast (Al Pacino, Robert Duval, Robert De Niro), Fredo Corleone (John Cazale) orders a Frozen Banana Daiquiri while in the Cuban capital.

INGREDIENTS

light or amber rum 1½ oz (4.5 cl)
lemon or lime juice ¾ oz (2.5 cl)
simple syrup ¾ oz (2.5 cl)
fresh banana 2½ oz (70 g) approx.

PREPARATION

Measure 1½ oz (4.5 cl) of light or amber rum in a jigger and pour into a blender. Repeat with ¾ oz (2.5 cl) of simple syrup and ¾ oz (2.5 cl) of lemon or lime juice. Add 2½ oz (70 g) approximately of fresh sliced banana and ½ tall tumbler of crushed ice, and blend for 15–20 seconds. Pour into a low tumbler and serve, garnishing with the remaining banana and 2 short straws.

SUGGESTED USE

A refreshing drink that will brighten up your summer days.

BATIDA DE LIMAO

Blending method

INGREDIENTS

cachaça 1½ oz
(4.5 cl)
freshly squeezed
lime juice 1½ oz (4.5 cl)
simple syrup ¾ oz (2.5 cl)
white or cane sugar 1 tbsp.
(20 g) approx.

PREPARATION

Measure 1½ oz (4.5 cl) of cachaça
in a jigger and pour it into a blender.
Repeat with 1½ oz (4.5 cl) of freshly
squeezed lime juice and ¾ oz (2.5
cl) of simple syrup. Add 1 tbsp. (20 g)
approximately of white or cane sugar
and ½ a tall tumbler of crushed ice.
Blend for 15–20 seconds and pour into
the tumbler. To serve, garnish with 1 lime
slice and 2 long straws.

SUGGESTED USE

A particularly fresh and thirst-quenching
drink.

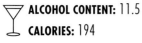
BATIDA DE MORANGO

Blending method

INGREDIENTS

cachaça 1 ½ oz (4.5 cl)
white or cane sugar 1 tbsp. (20 g)
approx.
fresh strawberries 5
strawberry puree ½ oz (1.5 cl)
simple syrup 1 oz (3 cl)

PREPARATION

Measure 1 ½ oz (4.5 cl) of cachaça in
a jigger and pour into a blender. Repeat
with 1 oz (3 cl) of simple syrup. Add
1 tbsp. (20 g) approximately of white or
cane sugar, 5 fresh strawberries, ½ oz
(1.5 cl) of strawberry puree (previously
measured in a jigger), and ½ a tall tumbler
of crushed ice. Blend for 15–20 seconds
and pour into the tumbler. Serve, garnished
with fresh strawberries and 2 long straws.

SUGGESTED USE

A great drink suitable for any time of day.

BLACK MOJITO

Muddler method

ALCOHOL CONTENT: 8.9
CALORIES: 146

INGREDIENTS

licorice liqueur 2 oz (6 cl)
½ lime
fresh mint ¼ oz (7 g) approx.
white or cane sugar 1 tbsp. (20 g)
approx.
soda water or sparkling water
2 oz (6 cl)

PREPARATION

Cut ½ a lime into cubes. Put the lime
cubes in a tall tumbler and add 1
tbsp. (20 g) approximately of white or
cane sugar. Grind everything with a
pestle until it is pulp. Add ¼ oz (7 g)
approximately of fresh mint and press
lightly. Fill the glass with crushed ice or
ice cubes and add 2 oz (6 cl) of licorice
liqueur (previously measured in a jigger).
Fill almost to the brim with 2 oz (6 cl) of
soda water or sparkling water and mix
with a long-handled spoon so that the
ingredients blend well. Serve, garnished
with 1 wheel of licorice, 1 nice sprig of
fresh mint, and 2 long straws.

SUGGESTED USE

A drink to enjoy throughout the day.

BLOODY BISHOP

Building method

INGREDIENTS
dry sherry 1½ oz (4.5 cl)
tomato juice 3 oz (9 cl)
lemon or lime juice ¾ oz (2.5 cl)
spices

PREPARATION
Measure 1½ oz (4.5 cl) of dry sherry in a jigger and pour into a tall tumbler. Repeat with ¾ oz (2.5 cl) of lemon or lime juice and 3 oz (9 cl) of tomato juice. Add salt, pepper, 1 dash (a few drops) of tabasco, 1 dash (a few drops) of Worcestershire sauce, and a few ice cubes. Stir all the ingredients vigorously with a long-handled spoon and serve garnished with 2 long straws, 1 slice of avocado, and 1 rib of celery (optional).

SUGGESTED USE
Excellent as an aperitif and for the early afternoon.

 ALCOHOL CONTENT: 8.6
CALORIES: 122

BLOODY MARIA

Muddler method

INGREDIENTS
tequila 1½ oz (4.5 cl)
tomato juice 3 oz (9 cl)
lemon juice ½ oz (1.5 cl)
spices

PREPARATION
Measure 1½ oz (4.5 cl) of tequila in a jigger and pour into a tall tumbler. Repeat with ½ oz (1.5 cl) of lemon juice and 3 oz (9 cl) of tomato juice. Add salt, pepper, a dash of Tabasco, Worcestershire sauce, jalapeño peppers, and some ice cubes. Mix the ingredients thoroughly with a long-handled spoon and serve, garnished with 1 slice of avocado, 1 celery stick (optional), and 2 long straws.

SUGGESTED USE
Perfect for happy hour and ideal to accompany Mexican cuisine.

ALCOHOL CONTENT: 15.8
CALORIES: 147

Everyone knows how much British 30-year-old Bridget Jones (Renée Zellweger) wishes to find her Prince Charming, and how much she loves food. However, few people know about her passion for spending her afternoons with friends watching old movies, gossiping, and drinking Bloody Marys. Thanks to this successful 2001 romantic comedy, this drink and its variantions became popular in Europe as well.

ALCOHOL CONTENT: 16.6
CALORIES: 268

BLUE ANGEL ICE

Blending method

INGREDIENTS

dry vodka 1 oz (3 cl)
Cointreau or triple sec ¾ oz (2.5 cl)
Blue Curaçao 1 oz (3 cl)
lemon or lime juice ¾ oz (2.5 cl)
lemon ice cream 5 ¼ oz (100 g)
approx.

PREPARATION

Measure 1 oz (3 cl) of dry vodka in a
jigger and pour into a blender. Repeat
with ¾ oz (2.5 cl) of Cointreau or triple
sec, 1 oz (3 cl) of Blue Curaçao, and ¾
oz (2.5 cl) of lemon or lime juice. Add 5
¼ oz (100 g) approximately of lemon ice
cream and ½ a low tumbler of crushed ice.
Blend for 15–20 seconds and pour into a
tall tumbler. Serve, garnished with ½ a slice
of orange, 3 cocktail cherries, and 2 long
straws.

SUGGESTED USE

A particularly thirst-quenching drink, it is also a
good digestif.

BRAZIL COLADA

Blending method

INGREDIENTS

cachaça 2 oz (6 cl)
pineapple juice 3 oz (9 cl)
coconut puree 1 oz (3 cl)
simple syrup ½ oz (1.5 cl)

PREPARATION

Measure 2 oz (6 cl) of cachaça in a
jigger and pour into a blender or food
processor. Repeat with 1 oz (3 cl) of
coconut puree, ½ oz (1.5 cl) of simple
syrup, and 3 oz (9 cl) of pineapple
juice. Add ½ a tall tumbler of crushed
ice and blend for 15–20 seconds. Pour
into the tumbler and serve, garnished
with ½ a slice of pineapple, 2 cocktail
cherries, and 2 long straws.

SUGGESTED USE

A perfect drink to liven up any time of day.

CAIPIRISSIMA

Muddler method

INGREDIENTS

light rum 2 oz (6 cl)
½ lime
white or cane sugar 1 tbsp. (20 g)
approx.

PREPARATION

Place ½ a lime, cut into cubes, in a
low tumbler. Add 1 tbsp. (20 g)
approximately of sugar and crush it
all with a pestle until it's pulp. Add
crushed ice and 2 oz (6 cl) of light rum
previously measured in a jigger. Stir
for a few seconds with a long-handled
spoon to best mix the ingredients. Serve,
garnished with 2 short straws.

SUGGESTED USE

An excellent refreshing drink enjoyable from
late morning until late at night.

CAIPIROSKA

Muddler method

INGREDIENTS

dry vodka 2 oz (6 cl)
½ lime
white or cane sugar 1 tbsp.
(20 g) approx.

PREPARATION

Cut ½ a lime into cubes, place
in a low tumbler, and add 1 tbsp.
(20 g) approximately of sugar. With
a pestle, crush it all up to make a
pulp. Fill the glass with crushed ice
and pour in 2 oz (6 cl) of dry vodka
previously measured in a jigger. Stir
for a few seconds with a long-handled
spoon to best mix the ingredients. Serve,
garnished with 2 short straws.

SUGGESTED USE

A perfect drink for happy hour, but to be
enjoyed in moderation.

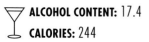

CANCHANCHARA

Building method or Shake and Pour

INGREDIENTS

dark rum 2 oz (6 cl)
lemon or lime juice ¾ oz (2.5 cl)
spiced apple syrup ¾ oz (2.5 cl)
sparkling water or soda water
1½ oz (4.5 cl) (optional)

PREPARATION

Measure 2 oz (6 cl) of dark rum in a jigger and pour into a low tumbler or a shaker. Repeat with ¾ oz (2.5 cl) of lemon or lime juice and ¾ oz (2.5 cl) of spiced apple syrup. Mix all the ingredients with no ice using a long-handled spoon or shake vigorously for a few seconds. Either way, pour into a low tumbler filled with ice. Optionally, add 1½ oz (4.5 cl) of sparkling water or soda water previously measured in a jigger. Serve garnished with a few lemon or lime wedges.

SUGGESTED USE

A particularly refreshing drink. Excellent to enjoy at any time of the day, it can also be served in a terra-cotta glass.

CHUPITO
(RUM AND PEAR SHOOTER)
Building method

ALCOHOL CONTENT: 8.6
CALORIES: 86

INGREDIENTS
dark rum 1 oz (3 cl)
pear juice 1 oz (3 cl)

PREPARATION
Measure 1 oz (3 cl) of dark rum in a jigger and pour into a shot glass (chupito). Repeat with 1 oz (3 cl) of pear juice in a second shot glass and serve.

SUGGESTED USE
Excellent after meals.

COSMOPOLITAN

Shake and Strain method

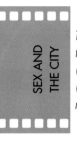

The Cosmopolitan is an undisputed protagonist of the HBO TV series that aired from 1998 to 2004, and of the 2008 movie adaptation. It is the favorite drink of Carrie Bradshaw (Sarah Jessica Parker) and her inseparable friends, Samantha (Kim Cattrall), Charlotte (Kristin Davis), and Miranda (Cynthia Nixon). This is fitting, as since its creation, this rose-colored cocktail has been associated with strong, modern women like Madonna.

INGREDIENTS

dry vodka 1¼ oz (4 cl)
Cointreau or triple sec ½ oz (1.5 cl)
lemon or lime juice ½ oz (1.5 cl)
cranberry juice 1 oz (3 cl)

PREPARATION

Measure 1¼ oz (4 cl) of dry vodka in a jigger and pour into a shaker. Repeat with ½ oz (1.5 cl) of Cointreau or triple sec, ½ oz (1.5 cl) of lemon or lime juice, and 1 oz (3 cl) of cranberry juice. Add some ice cubes and shake vigorously for a few seconds. Strain the drink into a chilled cocktail glass (previously chilled in the freezer), holding the ice back with the strainer, and serve.

SUGGESTED USE

Recommended as an evening cocktail or for happy hour.

COSMOPOLITAN ICE

Blending method

ALCOHOL CONTENT: 10.8
CALORIES: 204

INGREDIENTS

dry vodka 1½ oz (4.5 cl)
Cointreau or triple sec 1 oz (3 cl)
lemon ice cream 5¼ oz (100 g)
approx.
cranberry juice or syrup ¾ oz (2.5 cl)

PREPARATION

Measure 1½ oz (4.5 cl) of dry vodka
in a jigger and pour into a blender.
Repeat with 1 oz (3 cl) of Cointreau
or triple sec and ¾ oz (2.5 cl) of
cranberry juice or syrup. Add 5¼ oz
(100 g) approximately of lemon ice
cream and ½ a low tumbler of crushed
ice. Blend for 15–20 seconds and pour
into a tall tumbler. Serve, garnished with
some cocktail cherries and 2 long straws.

SUGGESTED USE

An excellent drink for the evening, it is
especially loved by women.

GASOLINA

Shake and Strain method

INGREDIENTS

pisco 1 oz (3 cl)
Blue Curaçao 1 oz (3 cl)
lemon or lime juice ¾ oz (2.5 cl)
simple syrup ½ oz (1.5 cl)
strawberry smoothie or juice 2 oz (6 cl)
gum nero syrup ⅙ oz (0.5 cl)

PREPARATION

Measure ⅙ oz (0.5 cl) of gum nero
syrup in a jigger and pour into a
shaker. Repeat with 1 oz (3 cl) of pisco,
1 oz (3 cl) of Blue Curaçao, ¾ oz (2.5
cl) of lemon or lime juice, ½ oz (1.5
cl) of simple syrup, and 2 oz (6 cl) of
strawberry smoothie or juice. Add a few
ice cubes and shake vigorously for a few
seconds. Holding the ice back with a
strainer, strain the drink into a tall tumbler
filled with ice and serve, garnished with
2 long straws.

SUGGESTED USE

A drink recommended for all hours of the
evening.

GIADA BLU
(BLUE JADE)
Shake and Strain method

ALCOHOL CONTENT: 12.3
CALORIES: 134

INGREDIENTS
Müller-Thurgau wine 1 oz (3 cl)
Cointreau or triple sec ¾ oz (2.5 cl)
Blue Curaçao ¾ oz (2.5 cl)
pineapple juice 3 oz (9 cl)
lemon or lime juice ½ oz (1.5 cl)

PREPARATION
Measure 1 oz (3 cl) of Müller-Thurgau wine in a jigger and pour into a shaker. Repeat with ¾ oz (2.5 cl) of Cointreau or triple sec, ¾ oz (2.5 cl) of Blue Curaçao, 3 oz (9 cl) of pineapple juice, and ½ oz (1.5 cl) of lemon or lime juice. Add a few ice cubes and shake vigorously for a few seconds. Holding the ice back with a strainer, strain the drink into a tall tumbler filled with ice and serve garnished with 2 long straws, ½ a slice of pineapple, and some red currants.

SUGGESTED USE
Strongly recommended for the hottest days.

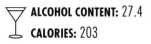

ITALIAN ICED TEA

Shake and Strain method

INGREDIENTS

white grappa ¾ oz (2.5 cl)

dry vodka ¾ oz (2.5 cl)

light rum ¾ oz (2.5 cl)

gin ¾ oz (2.5 cl)

lemon or lime juice ¾ oz (2.5 cl)

cola 1 oz (3 cl)

PREPARATION

Measure ¾ oz (2.5 cl) of white grappa in a jigger and pour into a shaker. Repeat with ¾ oz (2.5 cl) of dry vodka, ¾ oz (2.5 cl) of rum, ¾ oz (2.5 cl) of gin, and ¾ oz (2.5 cl) of lemon or lime juice. Shake vigorously for a few seconds then, holding the ice back with a strainer, strain the drink into a tall tumbler filled with ice. Fill almost to the brim with 1 oz (3 cl) of cola (previously measured in a jigger) and serve, garnished with 1 lemon slice, some cocktail cherries, and 2 long straws.

SUGGESTED USE

A long drink greatly appreciated by young people and to be enjoyed, in moderation, at all hours of the evening.

JAMAICA'S DREAM

Shake and Strain method

ALCOHOL CONTENT: 16.4

CALORIES: 297

INGREDIENTS

light rum 1 oz (3 cl)
dark rum 1 oz (3 cl)
Passoã liqueur 1 oz (3cl)
tropical juice 2 oz (6 cl)
mango puree ½ oz (1.5 cl)
papaya puree ½ oz (1.5 cl)
tropical fruit

PREPARATION

Measure 1 oz (3 cl) of dark rum in a jigger and pour into a shaker. Repeat with 1 oz (3 cl) of light rum, 1 oz (3 cl) of Passoã liqueur, 2 oz (6 cl) of tropical juice, ½ oz (1.5 cl) of papaya puree, and ½ oz (1.5 cl) of mango puree. Add some ice cubes and shake vigorously for a few seconds. Holding the ice back with a strainer, strain the drink into a large glass cup filled with ice. Cover with plenty of crushed ice and have fun decorating as desired, alternating slices of mango, papaya, passion fruit, pineapple, and banana. To serve, garnish with 2 long straws and some toothpicks.

SUGGESTED USE

This lively drink will delight your guests and can enliven every hour of the day and evening.

ALCOHOL CONTENT: 11.8
CALORIES: 186

JAMAICAN MOJITO

Muddler method

INGREDIENTS

dark or amber rum 2 oz (6 cl)
½ lime
white or cane sugar 1 tbsp. (20 g)
approx.
fresh mint ¼ oz (7 g) approx.
fresh fruit salad 2 oz (60 g) approx.
lime or lemon juice ½ oz (1.5 cl)
soda water or sparkling water 2 oz (6 cl)

PREPARATION

Put ½ a lime, cut into cubes, in a
large glass and add 1 tbsp. (20 g)
approximately of white or cane sugar.
Grind everything with a pestle until it is
pulp. Add ¼ oz (7 g) approximately of
fresh mint and press lightly against the glass.
Add 2 oz (60 g) approximately of fresh fruit
salad, 2 oz (6 cl) of dark or amber rum,
and ½ oz (1.5 cl) of lime or lemon juice
(previously measured in a jigger). Fill the glass
with crushed ice or ice cubes then fill almost
to the brim with 2 oz (6 cl) of soda water or
sparkling water. Mix everything with a long-
handled spoon so that the ingredients blend
well. To serve, garnish with 2 cocktail cherries,
½ a slice of pineapple on a long toothpick
(which can be used to grab the fruit), and 2
long straws.

SUGGESTED USE

A happy and visually stimulating drink that can
be enjoyed at all hours of the day.

KAMIKAZE

Shake and Strain method

ALCOHOL CONTENT: 20.8
CALORIES: 156

INGREDIENTS

dry vodka 1 oz (3 cl)
Cointreau or triple sec 1 oz (3 cl)
lemon or lime juice 1 oz (3 cl)

PREPARATION

Measure 1 oz (3 cl) of dry vodka in a
jigger and pour into a shaker. Repeat
with 1 oz (3 cl) of Cointreau or triple
sec and 1 oz (3 cl) of lemon or lime
juice. Add a few ice cubes and shake
vigorously for a few seconds. Strain the
drink in a cocktail glass (pre-chilled in
the freezer), holding the ice back with
the strainer.

SUGGESTED USE

Good as a digestif, this cocktail,
which is very high in alcohol content,
is especially recommended for lively
evenings at the nightclub.

LADY MOJITO ROSÉ

Muddler method

INGREDIENTS

dry vermouth 1½ oz (4.5 cl)
½ lime
white or cane sugar 1 tbsp.
(20 g) approx.
fresh mint ¼ oz (7 g) approx.
brut sparkling wine or rosé
Champagne 2 oz (6 cl)

PREPARATION

Cut ½ a lime into small cubes and
put it in a tall tumbler together with
1 tbsp. (20 g) approximately of white
or cane sugar. Grind everything with
a pestle until it is pulp. Add ¼ oz (7 g)
approximately of fresh mint and press
gently. Fill the glass with crushed ice
or ice cubes and add 1½ oz (4.5 cl)
of dry vermouth previously measured in
a jigger. Fill almost to the brim with 2
oz (6 cl) of brut sparkling wine or rosé
Champagne and stir gently with a long-
handled spoon. Serve garnished with
½ a passion fruit, 1 sprig of fresh mint,
and 2 long straws.

SUGGESTED USE

A great aperitif especially beloved by
female drinkers.

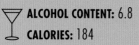

ALCOHOL CONTENT: 6.8
CALORIES: 184

LIQUAICE

Blending method

INGREDIENTS

licorice liqueur 2 oz (6 cl)
light rum 1½ oz (4.5 cl)
milk-flavored ice cream or vanilla ice
cream 5¼ oz (100 g) approx.

PREPARATION

Measure 2 oz (6 cl) of licorice liqueur
in a jigger and pour into a blender.
Repeat with 1½ oz (4.5 cl) of
light rum. Add 5¼ oz (100 g)
approximately of milk-flavored or vanilla
ice cream and ½ a low tumbler of
crushed ice. Blend for 15–20 seconds
and pour into a tall tumbler. To serve,
garnish with 2 wheels of licorice and
2 long straws.

SUGGESTED USE

An excellent after-dinner drink, also
recommended as a digestif.

ALCOHOL CONTENT: 22.3
CALORIES: 360

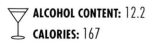

ALCOHOL CONTENT: 12.2
CALORIES: 167

MOJITO BASITO

Muddler method

INGREDIENTS

light or amber rum 2 oz (6 cl)
½ lime
fresh basil ¼ oz (7 g) approx.
white or cane sugar 1 tbsp. (20 g)
approx.
soda water or sparkling water 2 oz
(6 cl)

PREPARATION

Put ½ a lime, cut into cubes, in a
tall tumbler and add 1 tbsp. (20 g)
approximately of white or cane sugar.
Grind everything with a pestle until it is
pulp. Add ¼ oz (7 g) approximately
of fresh basil and press lightly against
the glass. Fill with crushed ice or ice
cubes and add 2 oz (6 cl) of light or
amber rum (previously measured in a
jigger). Fill almost to the brim with 2 oz
(6 cl) of soda water or sparkling water.
Mix everything with a long-handled spoon
so that the ingredients are well blended.
Serve, garnished with 1 sprig of fresh basil
and 2 long straws.

SUGGESTED USE

An extremely scented cocktail suitable for all
hours of the evening.

MOJITO FIDEL

Building method

ALCOHOL CONTENT: 18
CALORIES: 198

INGREDIENTS

light or amber rum 2 oz (6 cl)
lime juice 1 oz (3 cl) approx.
fresh mint ¼ oz (7 g) approx.
white or cane sugar 1 tbsp.
(20 g) approx.
lager beer 2 oz (6 cl)

PREPARATION

Measure 2 oz (6 cl) of light or
amber rum in a jigger and pour in a
tall tumbler. Repeat with 1 oz (3 cl)
approximately of lime juice. Combine
1 tbsp. (20 g) approximately of
white or cane sugar and ¼ oz (7 g)
approximately of fresh mint, and mix
everything with a long-handled spoon.
Fill the glass with ice roughly crushed or
in small cubes and fill almost to the brim
with 2 oz (6 cl) of lager beer (previously
measured in a jigger). Mix again, then
serve, garnished with 1 sprig of fresh mint
and 2 long straws.

SUGGESTED USE

A drink that can be enjoyed throughout
the evening, it is also recommended as an
aperitif.

ITALIAN MOJITO

Muddler method

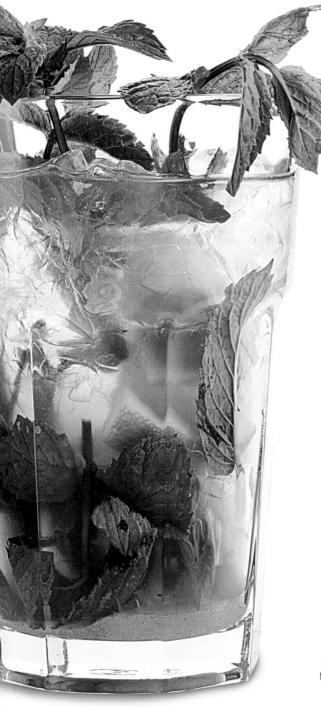

INGREDIENTS

white grappa 2 oz (6 cl)
½ lime
fresh mint ¼ oz (7 g) approx.
white or cane sugar 1 tbsp.
(20 g) approx.
soda water or sparkling water
2 oz (6 cl)

PREPARATION

Put ½ a lime, cut into small cubes,
in a tall tumbler and add 1 tbsp.
(20 g) approximately of white or
cane sugar. Grind everything with a
pestle until it is pulp. Add ¼ oz
(7 g) approximately of fresh mint,
gently pressing it down. Fill the tumbler
with crushed ice or ice cubes and add
2 oz (6 cl) of white grappa (previously
measured in a jigger). Fill almost to the
brim with 2 oz (6 cl) of soda water or
sparkling mineral water. Stir with a long-
handled spoon so as to best blend the
ingredients. Serve, garnished with a nice
sprig of mint and 2 long straws.

SUGGESTED USE

A great drink that can be enjoyed
throughout the evening.

MOJITO ROYAL

Muddler method

INGREDIENTS

light or amber rum 2 oz (6 cl)
½ lime
fresh mint ¼ oz (7 g) approx.
brut sparkling wine 2 oz (6 cl)
white or cane sugar 1 tbsp. (20 g)
approx.

PREPARATION

Put ½ lime, cut into cubes, in a tall
tumbler and add 1 tbsp. (20 g)
approximately of white or cane sugar.
Grind everything with a pestle until it is
a pulp. Add ¼ oz (7 g) approximately
of fresh mint and press lightly against
the glass. Fill with crushed ice or ice
cubes and add 2 oz (6 cl) of light or
amber rum (previously measured in a
jigger). Fill almost to the brim with 2 oz (6
cl) of brut sparkling wine and mix with a
long-handled spoon so that the ingredients
blend well. To serve, garnish with 1 sprig
of fresh mint, ½ an orange slice, and 2
long straws.

SUGGESTED USE

An excellent aperitif.

ALCOHOL CONTENT: 17.8
CALORIES: 218

MONTECARLO

Shake and Strain method

INGREDIENTS

brut Chardonnay wine or Champagne 2 oz
(6 cl)
freshly squeezed orange juice
1 oz (3 cl)
raspberry puree 1 oz (3 cl)
Cointreau or triple sec 1 oz (3 cl)

PREPARATION

Measure 1 oz (3 cl) of Cointreau or triple
sec in a jigger and pour into a shaker.
Repeat with 1 oz (3 cl) of freshly squeezed
orange juice and 1 oz (3 cl) of raspberry
puree. Add some ice cubes and shake
vigorously for a few seconds. Holding
the ice back with a strainer, strain the
drink into a wine glass and fill with
2 oz (6 cl) of brut Chardonnay wine
or Champagne.

SUGGESTED USE

An excellent aperitif, but also
enjoyable at any other time of the
day.

ALCOHOL CONTENT: 11.3
CALORIES: 87

ALCOHOL CONTENT: 14.2
CALORIES: 179

MOSCOW MULE
Building method

INGREDIENTS
dry vodka 1½ oz (4.5 cl)
ginger beer 4 oz (12 cl)
lemon or lime juice ½ oz (1.5 cl)

PREPARATION
Measure 1½ oz (4.5 cl) of dry vodka in a jigger and pour into a low tumbler or a mug filled with ice. Repeat with 4 oz (12 cl) of ginger beer and ½ oz (1.5 cl) of lemon or lime juice. Stir for a few seconds with a long-handled spoon and serve, garnished with 2 lemon or lime wedges and 2 short straws.

SUGGESTED USE
A must for contemporary aperitifs.

ORANGE JAM CAIPIRITA

Muddler method

ALCOHOL CONTENT: 16.4
CALORIES: 244

INGREDIENTS

tequila 2 oz (6 cl)
white or cane sugar 1 tbsp. (20 g)
approx.
½ lime
orange marmalade 2½ tbsp.
(50 g) approx.
simple syrup ¾ oz (2.5 cl)

PREPARATION

Put ½ a diced lime in a glass jar
and add 1 tbsp. (20 g)
approximately of white sugar. Grind
everything with the help of a pestle until
it's pulp. Combine 2½ tbsp. (50 g)
approximately of orange marmalade,
2 oz (6 cl) of tequila, and ¾ oz (2.5 cl)
of simple syrup previously measured in a
jigger. Fill the jar with some crushed ice
and stir vigorously for a few seconds with
a long-handled spoon. Serve, garnished
with 2 short straws.

SUGGESTED USE

A young drink that can be enjoyed at all
hours of the evening. The use of orange
marmalade is one choice. You can replace
it with whatever marmalade you
like best.

ORIENTAL PEACH

Blending method

INGREDIENTS

dry vermouth 1¼ oz (4 cl)
peach puree 2 oz (6 cl)
orange juice 2 oz (6 cl)
ground cinnamon ½ tsp.

PREPARATION

Measure 1¼ oz (4 cl) of dry
vermouth in a jigger and pour into
a blender. Repeat with 2 oz (6 cl)
of peach puree and 2 oz (6 cl) of
orange juice. Add ½ a teaspoon of
ground cinnamon, ½ a low tumbler
of crushed ice, and blend for 15–20
seconds. Pour into a tall tumbler and
serve, garnished with 2 long straws, 3
orange wedges, and 1 cocktail cherry.

SUGGESTED USE

Ideal for those who love spiced drinks to
enjoy throughout the day.

ORIGINAL CUBAN MOJITO

Building method

ALCOHOL CONTENT: 11.6

CALORIES: 160

Released in 2006 and directed by the talented Michael Mann, this successful remake of the 1980s' TV series of the same name made the Original Cuban Mojito known all over the world. This drink has always been beloved in Florida, and among its loyal followers is the character of Sonny Crockett (Colin Farrell), as he himself testifies in one of his lines.

MIAMI VICE

INGREDIENTS

lime juice 1 oz (3 cl)
fresh mint* ¼ oz (7 g) approx.
white sugar** or white cane sugar
1 tbsp. (20 g) approx.
light or amber rum 1½ oz (4.5 cl)
soda water or sparkling water 2 oz (6 cl)

PREPARATION

Measure 1½ oz (4.5 cl) of light or amber rum in a jigger and pour into a tall tumbler. Repeat with 1 oz (3 cl) of freshly squeezed lime juice. Combine 1 tbsp. (20 g) approximately of white or white cane sugar and ¼ oz (7 g) approximately of fresh mint, then mix everything with a long-handled spoon. Fill the glass with roughly crushed ice or ice cubes and fill almost to the brim with 2 oz (6 cl) of soda water or sparkling water. Give a final stir and serve, garnishing with 1 sprig of fresh mint and 2 long straws.

SUGGESTED USE

The Mojito is the best-known Cuban aperitif in the world.
* In Cuba it is prepared with hierba buena
**In Cuba it is prepared with white cane sugar

ALCOHOL CONTENT: 6.8
CALORIES: 228

PASSION MOJITO

Muddler method

INGREDIENTS

Passoã 2 oz (6 cl)
½ lime
white or cane sugar
1 tbsp. (20 g) approx.
fresh mint ¼ oz (7 g)
approx.
soda water or sparkling
water 2 oz (6 cl)
passion fruit

PREPARATION

Cut ½ a lime into cubes. Put the lime
in a tall tumbler and add 1 tbsp.
(20 g) approximately of white or
cane sugar. Grind everything with a
pestle until it is pulp. Add ¼ oz (7 g)
approximately of fresh mint and press
lightly. Fill the glass with crushed ice
or ice cubes and pour 2 oz (6 cl) of
Passoã (previously measured in a jigger).
Fill almost to the brim with 2 oz (6 cl) of
soda water or sparkling water and mix
with a long-handled spoon so that the
ingredients blend well. Serve, garnished
with ½ a passion fruit, 1 sprig of fresh
mint, and 2 long straws.

SUGGESTED USE

A delicious drink that can be enjoyed
throughout the evening. It is especially
popular among female drinkers.

PEPITO COLLINS

Building method

INGREDIENTS

tequila 1½ oz (4.5 cl)
lemon or lime juice 1 oz (3 cl)
simple syrup ¾ oz (2.5 cl)
soda water or sparkling water
2 oz (6 cl)

PREPARATION

Measure 1½ oz (4.5 cl) of tequila in
a jigger and pour into a tall tumbler
filled with ice. Repeat with 1 oz (3 cl)
of lemon or lime juice, ¾ oz (2.5 cl) of
simple syrup, and 2 oz (6 cl) of soda
water or sparkling water. Stir gently
for a few seconds with a long-handled
spoon and serve, garnished with
a slice of lemon, some cocktail cherries,
and 2 long straws.

SUGGESTED USE

An excellent refreshing long drink that can
be served at all hours of the day.

FROZEN PICK-ME-UP

Blending method

INGREDIENTS

egg liqueur 1 oz (3 cl)
chocolate liqueur 1 oz (3 cl)
coffee liqueur 1 oz (3 cl)
milk-flavored or vanilla ice cream
2¾ oz (50 g) approx.

PREPARATION

Measure 1 oz (3 cl) of egg liqueur
in a jigger and pour it into a
blender. Repeat with 1 oz (3 cl) of
chocolate liqueur and 1 oz (3 cl) of
coffee liqueur. Add the ice cream and
½ tall tumbler of crushed ice, then
blend for 15–20 seconds. Pour into a
low tumbler and serve, garnished with
2 short straws and a dusting of cocoa.

SUGGESTED USE

Perfect as an after-dinner drink, but also
good as a digestif.

PINK COLADA

Blending method

INGREDIENTS
light rum 1½ oz (4.5 cl)
pineapple juice 3 oz (9 cl)
coconut puree ½ oz (1.5 cl)
grenadine syrup ¾ oz (2.5 cl)

PREPARATION
Measure 1½ oz (4.5 cl) of light rum
in a jigger and pour into a blender.
Repeat with 3 oz (9 cl) of pineapple
juice, ½ oz (1.5 cl) of coconut puree,
and ¾ oz (2.5 cl) of grenadine syrup.
Add ½ a tall tumbler of crushed ice and
blend for 15–20 seconds. Pour into the
tumbler and serve, garnished with ½ a
slice of pineapple, 2 cocktail cherries,
and 2 long straws.

SUGGESTED USE
A drink with strong energy-boosting
properties.

ALCOHOL CONTENT: 14.9
CALORIES: 142

PISCO COLLINS

Shake and Strain method

INGREDIENTS

pisco 2 oz (6 cl)
simple syrup ½ oz (1.5 cl)
lemon or lime juice 1 oz (3 cl)
soda water or sparkling water 2 oz
(6 cl)

PREPARATION

Measure 2 oz (6 cl) of pisco in a
jigger and pour into a shaker. Repeat
with 1 oz (3 cl) of lemon or lime juice
and ½ oz (1.5 cl) of simple syrup. Add
a few ice cubes and shake vigorously
for a few seconds. Holding the ice
back with a strainer, strain the drink
into a tall tumbler filled with ice and fill
almost to the brim with 2 oz (6 cl) of
soda water or sparkling water. Stir with a
long-handled spoon and serve, garnished
with ½ a slice of lemon, 2 cocktail
cherries, and 2 long straws.

SUGGESTED USE

A drink with marked thirst-quenching
properties.

PISCO PASSION

Shake and Strain method

ALCOHOL CONTENT: 12.8
CALORIES: 180

INGREDIENTS

pisco 1 oz (3 cl)
Passoã 1 oz (3 cl)
lemon or lime juice 1 oz (3 cl)
passion fruit 1
passion fruit puree ½ oz (1.5 cl)

PREPARATION

Measure 1 oz (3 cl) of pisco in a jigger
and pour into a shaker. Repeat with 1 oz
(3 cl) of lemon or lime juice, 1 oz (3 cl) of
Passoã, and ½ oz (1.5 cl) of passion fruit
puree. Add a few ice cubes and the pulp
from ½ a passion fruit, then shake it all for
a few seconds. Holding the ice back with a
strainer, strain the drink into a cocktail glass
(pre-chilled in the freezer) and serve, garnished
with the remaining passion fruit.

SUGGESTED USE

A drink best enjoyed among good company.
It is also recommended as a digestif.

PISCO SOUR

Shake and Strain method

INGREDIENTS

pisco 1½ oz (4.5 cl)
lemon or lime juice ¾ oz (2.5 cl)
simple syrup ½ oz (1.5 cl)

PREPARATION

Measure 1½ oz (4.5 cl) of pisco
in a jigger and pour into a shaker.
Repeat with ¾ oz (2.5 cl) of lemon or
lime juice and ½ oz (1.5 cl) of sugar
syrup. Add a few ice cubes and shake
vigorously for a few seconds. Holding
the ice back with a strainer, strain the
drink into a glass (pre-chilled in the
freezer) and serve.

SUGGESTED USE

An excellent digestif that can also be
enjoyed throughout the evening.

PISCO SUNRISE

Building method

ALCOHOL CONTENT: 16.2

CALORIES: 184

INGREDIENTS

pisco 2 oz (6 cl)
orange juice 3 oz (9 cl)
grenadine syrup ¾ oz (2.5 cl)

PREPARATION

Measure 2 oz (6 cl) of pisco in a
jigger and pour into a tall tumbler
filled with ice. Repeat with 3 oz (9
cl) of orange juice, then stir for a few
seconds with a long-handled spoon.
Measure ¾ oz (2.5 cl) of grenadine
syrup in a jigger and pour it slowly
into the tumbler, using the edge of the
spoon, until it reaches the bottom,
thus obtaining the rising sun effect.
Serve garnished with 2 orange slices,
2 cocktail cherries, and 2 long straws.

SUGGESTED USE

A great drink for the whole day, especially
when it is hot.

ALCOHOL CONTENT: 14.8
CALORIES: 162

PISCOLA
Building method

INGREDIENTS
pisco 2 oz (6 cl)
cola 4 oz (12 cl)

PREPARATION
Measure 4 oz (12 cl) of cola in a
jigger and pour into a tall tumbler
filled with ice. Combine 2 oz (6 cl) of
pisco using the edge of the spoon so
that it gives the appearance that it is
floating, and serve garnished with 2
long straws.

SUGGESTED USE
A drink recommended for very hot
days.

PUFFO ICE

Blending method

ALCOHOL CONTENT: 0
CALORIES: 260

INGREDIENTS

milk 3 oz (9 cl)
milk-flavored ice cream 5¼ oz
(100 g) approx.
Blue Curaçao syrup ¾ oz (2.5 cl)

PREPARATION

Measure 3 oz (9 cl) of milk in
a jigger and pour into a blender.
Repeat with ¾ oz (2.5 cl) of Blue
Curaçao syrup. Add 5¼ oz (100
g) approximately of milk-flavored
ice cream and ½ a low tumbler of
crushed ice. Blend for 15 seconds
and pour into a tall tumbler. To serve,
garnish with 2 long straws.

SUGGESTED USE

A nice soft drink that can quench your
children's thirst.

ALCOHOL CONTENT: 15.8
CALORIES: 480

SABBIA D'ORIENTE
(EASTERN SAND)

Blending method

INGREDIENTS

coffee liqueur 1 oz (3 cl)
Baileys 2 oz (6 cl)
milk-flavored ice cream or vanilla ice
cream 5¼ oz (100 g) approx.

PREPARATION

Measure 2 oz (6 cl) of Baileys in a
jigger and pour into a blender. Repeat
with 1 oz (3 cl) of coffee liqueur. Add
5¼ oz (100 g) approximately of milk-
flavored or vanilla ice cream and ½ a
low tumbler of crushed ice. Blend for
15–20 seconds and pour into a tall
tumbler. To serve, garnish with 2 long
straws and a dusting of cocoa.

SUGGESTED USE

A delightful dessert drink.

SHERRY POLITAN

Shake and Strain method

INGREDIENTS
dry sherry 1 oz (3 cl)
Cointreau or triple sec ¾ oz (2.5 cl)
lemon or lime juice ½ oz (1.5 cl)
cranberry juice 1 oz (3 cl)

PREPARATION
Measure 1 oz (3 cl) of dry sherry in a
jigger and pour into a shaker. Repeat
with ¾ oz (2.5 cl) of Cointreau or
triple sec, ½ oz (1.5 cl) of lemon or
lime juice,and 1 oz (3 cl) of cranberry
juice. Add a few ice cubes and shake
vigorously for a few seconds. Holding
the ice back with a strainer, strain the
drink into a cocktail glass pre-chilled in
the freezer and serve garnished with a
bunch of red currants.

SUGGESTED USE
A special digestive cocktail, suitable
for all hours of the day as well.

ALCOHOL CONTENT: 8.9
CALORIES: 192

SPRITZ MOJITO

Muddler method

INGREDIENTS

Aperol 2 oz (6 cl)
¼ fresh orange
white or cane sugar 1 tbsp. (20 g)
approx.
brut sparkling wine 2 oz (6 cl)
fresh mint ¼ oz (7 g) approx.
soda water or sparkling water ½ oz
(1.5 cl)

PREPARATION

Put ¼ of an orange, cut into cubes, in a tall tumbler and add 1 tbsp. (20 g) approximately of white or cane sugar. Grind everything with a pestle until it is pulp. Add ¼ oz (7 g) approximately of fresh mint and press lightly. Fill the glass with crushed ice or ice cubes and add 2 oz (6 cl) of Aperol (previously measured in a jigger). Repeat with 2 oz (6 cl) of brut sparkling wine and ½ oz (1.5 cl) of soda water or sparkling water. Mix everything with a long-handled spoon so that the ingredients blend well. To serve, garnish with 1 orange wedge, 1 sprig of fresh mint, and 2 long straws.

SUGGESTED USE

An excellent aperitif that can be enjoyed throughout the evening.

STRAWBERRY CAIPIROSKA

Muddler method

ALCOHOL CONTENT: 16.5
CALORIES: 216

INGREDIENTS

dry vodka 2 oz (6 cl)
fresh strawberries 3–4
½ lime
white or cane sugar 1 tbsp.
(20 g) approx.
strawberry puree ¾ oz (2.5 cl)

PREPARATION

Dice ½ a lime and place it in a
low tumbler. Add 1 tbsp. (20 g)
approximately of sugar, ¾ oz (2.5
cl) of strawberry puree, and 3–4
fresh strawberries. Grind everything
with a pestle until it is pulp.
Add crushed ice and 2 oz (6 cl) of
dry vodka previously measured in a
jigger. Stir for a few seconds with a
long-handled spoon to best mix the
ingredients. Serve, garnished with
2 short straws and some beautiful fresh
strawberries.

SUGGESTED USE

This drink is well loved by younger
drinkers, who typically choose it for their
happy hour.

STRAWBERRY DAIQUIRI ICE

Blending method

INGREDIENTS

light rum 2 oz (6 cl)
lemon ice cream 5¼ oz (100 g)
approx.
simple syrup 1 oz (3 cl)
fresh strawberries 5–6
lemon or lime juice ½ oz (1.5 cl)

PREPARATION

Measure 2 oz (6 cl) of light rum in a
jigger and pour into a blender. Repeat
with 1 oz (3 cl) of simple syrup and ½
oz (1.5 cl) of lemon or lime juice. Add
5¼ oz (100 g) approximately of lemon
ice cream, 5–6 fresh strawberries, and
½ a low tumbler of crushed ice. Blend
for 15–20 seconds and pour into a tall
tumbler. Serve, garnished with 2 nice
strawberries and 2 long straws.

SUGGESTED USE

An excellent digestif, recommended
throughout the day.

FROZEN STRAWBERRY MARGARITA

ALCOHOL CONTENT: 10.2
CALORIES: 122

Blending method

INGREDIENTS

clear tequila 1½ oz (4.5 cl)
Cointreau or triple sec ¾ oz (2.5 cl)
lemon or lime juice ½ oz (1.5 cl)
strawberry puree 1 oz (3 cl)
fresh strawberries 3–4

PREPARATION

Measure 1½ oz (4.5 cl) of clear
tequila in a jigger and pour it into
a blender or food processor. Repeat
with ¾ oz (2.5 cl) of Cointreau or
triple sec, ½ oz (1.5 cl) of lemon
or lime juice, and 1 oz (3 cl) of
strawberry puree. Add 3–4 fresh
strawberries and 1 tall tumbler of
crushed ice, then blend it all for 15–20
seconds. Pour into a low tumbler and
garnish with a few fresh strawberries
and 2 long straws.

SUGGESTED USE

A great refreshing drink, recommended for
all times of the day.

SWEET DREAM

Shake and Strain method

INGREDIENTS

dry vermouth 1½ oz (4.5 cl)
orange juice 1½ oz (4.5 cl)
Grand Marnier ½ oz (1.5 cl)

PREPARATION

Measure 1½ oz (4.5 cl) of dry
vermouth in a jigger and pour into
a shaker. Repeat with 1½ oz (4.5
cl) of orange juice and ½ oz (1.5
cl) of Grand Marnier. Add a few ice
cubes and shake vigorously for a few
seconds. Holding the ice back with a
strainer, strain the drink into a cocktail
glass pre-chilled in the freezer, then
serve, garnished with 4 cocktail cherries
tied onto a skewer.

SUGGESTED USE

A particularly aromatic aperitif that can
be enjoyed at all hours of the day.

ALCOHOL CONTENT: 10.6
CALORIES: 64

SWEET WATERMELON

Building method

INGREDIENTS

Brachetto wine 1 oz (3 cl)
Biancosarti liqueur 1 oz (3 cl)
sparkling water or soda water
1 oz (3 cl)

PREPARATION

Measure 1 oz (3 cl) of Brachetto wine in a
jigger and pour into a wine glass filled with
ice. Repeat with 1 oz (3 cl) of Biancosarti
liqueur. Fill almost to the brim with 1 oz
(3 cl) of sparkling water or soda water.
Stir gently with a long-handled spoon
and serve garnished with a skewer of
watermelon chunks.

SUGGESTED USE

An excellent aperitif, but also great to
enjoy throughout the day.

ALCOHOL CONTENT: 6.8
CALORIES: 48

TEQUILA BUM BUM

Building method

INGREDIENTS

tequila 1 oz (3 cl)
clear soda water (sparkling water,
tonic, club soda, etc.) 1 oz (3 cl)

PREPARATION

Measure 1 oz (3 cl) of tequila in a
jigger and pour into a shot glass with
a thick bottom. Repeat with 1 oz (3 cl)
of transparent soda water. Cover the
glass with a paper towel and slam (quite
forcefully) 2–3 times on a hard surface,
then serve.

SUGGESTED USE

A great drink for after dinner or late evening.

TEQUILA PUERTO VALLARTA

Building method

ALCOHOL CONTENT: 13.8
CALORIES: 152

INGREDIENTS

tequila 2 oz (6 cl)
orange juice 3 oz (9 cl)
lime or lemon juice ¾ oz (2.5 cl)
grenadine syrup ½ oz (1.5 cl)

PREPARATION

Measure 2 oz (6 cl) of tequila
in a jigger and pour into a tall
tumbler filled with ice. Repeat with
3 oz (9 cl) of orange juice, ¾ oz
(2.5 cl) of lime or lemon juice, and
½ oz (1.5 cl) of grenadine syrup. Stir
with a long-handled spoon and serve,
garnished with ½ a slice of lime,
2 cocktail cherries, and 2 long straws.

SUGGESTED USE

This refreshing drink is recommended for
all hours of the day.

TESTAROSSA ICE

Blending method

INGREDIENTS

dry vodka 1½ oz (4.5 cl)
bitter (Campari bitter is
recommended) 1½ oz (4.5 cl)
strawberry ice cream 5¼ oz
(100 g) approx.

PREPARATION

Measure 1½ oz (4.5 cl) of dry vodka
in a jigger and pour into a blender.
Repeat with 1½ oz (4.5 cl) of bitter.
Add 5¼ oz (100 g) approximately
of strawberry ice cream and ½ a low
tumbler of crushed ice. Blend for 15–20
seconds and pour into a tall tumbler.
To serve, garnish with 2 strawberries
and 2 long straws.

SUGGESTED USE

An excellent aperitif.

TOMMY'S MARGARITA

Shake and Strain method

ALCOHOL CONTENT: 10.2
CALORIES: 122

INGREDIENTS

light tequila 2 oz (6 cl)
lemon or lime juice ¾ oz (2.5 cl)
agave syrup ½ oz (1.5 cl)

PREPARATION

Measure 2 oz (6 cl) of light tequila
in a jigger and pour into a shaker.
Repeat with ¾ oz (2.5 cl) of lemon or
lime juice and ½ oz (1.5 cl) of agave
syrup. Add a few ice cubes and shake
vigorously for a few seconds. Holding
the ice back with a strainer, strain the
drink into a cocktail glass previously
chilled in the freezer and serve.

SUGGESTED USE

Excellent to enjoy at all hours.

ALCOHOL CONTENT: 18.6
CALORIES: 196

TORO LOCO
Building method

Coyote Ugly, the New York bar portrayed in this movie, is known for two things: the sensual dances with which the barmaids entertain the bar's patrons, and the Toro Loco, a drink the ladies successfully ply on their customers. Thanks to her job at the bar, Violet (Piper Perabo), an aspiring songwriter, manages not only to overcome her stage fright, but also finds love. Released in 2000, this movie became a global cultural phenomenon.

INGREDIENTS
mezcal 1 ½ oz (4.5 cl)
coffee liqueur 1 ½ oz (4.5 cl)

PREPARATION
Measure 1 ½ oz (4.5 cl) of mezcal in a jigger and pour into a low tumbler filled with ice. Repeat with 1 ½ oz (4.5 cl) of coffee liqueur. Stir with a long-handled spoon and serve garnished with 2 short straws.

SUGGESTED USE
An excellent digestif that is especially appreciated by male drinkers.

TROPICAL ICE

Blending method

INGREDIENTS

mint syrup ¾ oz (2.5 cl)
orgeat syrup ½ oz (1.5 cl)
milk-flavored ice cream
5¼ oz (100 g) approx.
milk 2 oz (6 cl)

PREPARATION

Measure 2 oz (6 cl) of milk in
a jigger and pour into a blender.
Repeat with ¾ oz (2.5 cl) of
mint syrup and ½ oz (1.5 cl) of
orgeat syrup. Add 5¼ oz (100 g)
approximately of milk-flavored ice
cream and ½ a low tumbler of crushed
ice. Blend for 15–20 seconds and pour
into a tall tumbler. To serve, garnish with
1 nice sprig of fresh mint and 2 long
straws.

SUGGESTED USE

A greatly refreshing drink, it is also suitable
for children.

VICTORIAN MOJITO

Muddler method

INGREDIENTS

gin 1 ½ oz (4.5 cl)
½ lime
white or cane sugar 1 tbsp.
(20 g) approx.
fresh mint ¼ oz (7 g) approx.
brut sparkling wine 2 oz (6 cl)

PREPARATION

Cut ½ a lime into cubes. Put the lime cubes in a tall tumbler and add 1 tbsp. (20 g) approximately of white or cane sugar. Grind everything with a pestle until it is pulp. Add ¼ oz (7 g) approximately of fresh mint leaves and press lightly. Fill the glass with crushed ice or ice cubes and add 1 ½ oz (4.5 cl) of gin (previously measured in a jigger). Fill almost to the brim with 2 oz (6 cl) of fresh brut sparkling wine and mix everything with a long-handled spoon so that the ingredients blend well. To serve, garnish with 1 nice sprig of fresh mint and 2 long straws.

SUGGESTED USE

An excellent aperitif that can be enjoyed throughout the evening.

VODKA SOUR PASSION

Shake and Strain method

ALCOHOL CONTENT: 14.4
CALORIES: 143

INGREDIENTS

dry vodka 1 oz (3 cl)
lemon or lime juice ¾ oz (2.5 cl)
Passoã liqueur ¾ oz (2.5 cl)
passion fruit puree ½ oz (1.5 cl)

PREPARATION

Measure 1 oz (3 cl) of dry vodka in a
jigger and pour into a shaker. Repeat
with ¾ oz (2.5 cl) of lemon or lime
juice, ¾ oz (2.5 cl) of Passoã, and
½ oz (1.5 cl) of passion fruit puree.
Add some ice cubes and shake for a
few seconds. Strain the drink into a glass
pre-chilled in the freezer, holding the ice
back with the strainer.

SUGGESTED USE

Commonly considered an aphrodisiac,
it is a digestive drink loved by young
people and most often consumed during
the evening for relaxation and fun.

HOT DRINKS & COFFEE

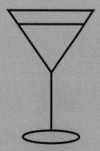

The origins of coffee are very ancient and uncertain, but according to the most accredited legend, it was accidentally discovered in the Ethiopian region of Kaffa in 850 CE by a shepherd named Kaldi. While grazing, his goats began to eat the leaves of the shrubs with which he was about to start a fire. During the night, Kaldi noticed that the animals, instead of falling asleep, were unusually hyperactive. After having understood what might have caused that state of restlessness, the shepherd toasted the red berries of the same plant on the fire, ground them, and then used them to prepare an infusion.

From then on, the spread of coffee became unstoppable, and it seems that as early as the 15th century, in present-day Yemen, rudimental cafés were incorporated in some monasteries.

Starting from the 16th century, this beverage became widespread all over the Middle East and North Africa, and it then arrived in Europe via the Ottoman Empire.

Around 1720, the first coffee plant appeared in the French colony of Martinique, and in 1927 plantations started in Brazil, which is now the main exporter of coffee in the world.

Today coffee is the second most consumed beverage in the world. Its caloric intake is almost nonexistent, and most people do not know that it is listed on the stock market. Its versatility has turned it into the absolute protagonist of cafés, patisseries and, more recently, of cuisine.

The invigorating effect of coffee is excellent if combined with various spirits while still hot. The most striking example is Irish Coffee, created in Ireland in 1943 by Joe Sheridan, a chef at an Irish restaurant near Foynes airport.

The use of coffee in cold drinks is becoming more and more frequent and fascinating. Among these, special praise is reserved for the lively Brazilian Batida and the Espresso Martini, a refined drink that has become extremely fashionable over the last decade.

As mentioned above, coffee is turning into a protagonist also in cuisine, thanks to innovative and sophisticated recipes that mostly combine it with game and red meat.

CARIBBEAN COFFEE

Building method

INGREDIENTS
dark rum 1½ oz (4.5 cl)
coffee liqueur ¾ oz (2.5 cl)
cane or white sugar 1 tbsp. (20 g)
approx.
hot coffee 3 oz (9 cl)
cream 2 oz (6 cl)

PREPARATION
Measure 1½ oz (4.5 cl) of dark rum
in a jigger and pour it into a metal
milk jug, repeating with ¾ oz (2.5
cl) of coffee liqueur. Combine 1 tbsp.
(20 g) approximately of sugar and 3
oz (9 cl) of hot coffee. Heat everything
up, stirring occasionally and being
careful not to exceed 158°F (70°C).
Pour into a heat-resistant mug and, just
before serving, add 2 oz (6 cl) of cream
(previously measured in a jigger), using
the edge of the teaspoon so that it remains
separate from the rest.

SUGGESTED USE
A drink with strong tonic properties, it is
recommended during the cooler times of the
year.

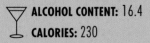
ALCOHOL CONTENT: 16.4
CALORIES: 230

FRENCH COFFEE

Building method

INGREDIENTS
cognac 1½ oz (4.5 cl)
coffee liqueur ¾ oz (2.5 cl)
cane or white sugar 1 tbsp. (20 g)
approx.
hot coffee 3 oz (9 cl)
cream 2 oz (6 cl)

PREPARATION
Measure 1½ oz (4.5 cl) of cognac in
a jigger and ¾ oz (2.5 cl) of coffee
liqueur and pour them into a milk jug.
Add 3 oz (9 cl) of hot coffee and 1 tbsp.
(20 g) approximately of white or cane
sugar. Heat everything up, stirring
occasionally and being careful not to
exceed 158°F (70°C) and pour into a
heat-resistant mug. Just before serving, add 2
oz (6 cl) of cream (previously measured in a
jigger) using the edge of a teaspoon so that it
remains separate from the rest.

SUGGESTED USE
To drink during the winter season: Your
excursions in the mountains or on ski slopes
will benefit from the powerful energy and
invigorating qualities of this fine hot drink.

GROG

Building method

The valuable energizing and healthy properties of this hot drink were already well-known during the Napoleonic Wars. An orderly of Captain Jack Aubrey (Russell Crowe), in a scene from 2003's Master and Commander, suggests to his superior that at a party one should never show up with wine, but rather with some Grog.

INGREDIENTS

dark rum 1½ oz (4.5 cl)
cane or white sugar 1 tbsp. (20 g) approx.
still water 2 oz (6 cl)
small cubes of lemon
small cubes of orange
cloves
cinnamon

PREPARATION

Measure 1½ oz (4.5 cl) of dark rum in a jigger and pour into a milk jug. Repeat with 2 oz (6 cl) of still water. Combine 5–6 cloves, 3 lemon cubes, 3 orange cubes, a cinnamon stick, and 1 tbsp. (20 g) approximately of sugar. Heat everything up, stirring occasionally and being careful not to exceed 158°F (70°C), then serve in a heat-resistant mug.

SUGGESTED USE

A drink with excellent invigorating properties and an effective remedy for stomach pains.

GROLLA VALDOSTANA

Building method

ALCOHOL CONTENT: 18.9

CALORIES: 280

INGREDIENTS

white grappa 1½ oz (4.5 cl)
Genepy liqueur (optional) ¾ oz (2.5 cl)
red wine 2 oz (6 cl)
coffee 2 oz (6 cl)
white or cane sugar 1 tbsp. (20 g) approx.
cloves
lemon peel
orange peel
juniper berries
orange punch, Cointreau, or triple sec
¾ oz (2.5 cl)

PREPARATION

Measure 1½ oz (4.5 cl) of white grappa
in a jigger and pour into a milk jug.
Repeat with 2 oz (6 cl) of red wine, ¾ oz
(2.5 cl) of Genepy liqueur, and ¾ oz (2.5
cl) of orange punch, Cointreau, or triple
sec. Add 2 oz (6 cl) of coffee (previously
measured in a jigger), 1 tbsp. (20 g)
approximately of white or cane sugar, 4–5
cloves, 2–3 lemon peels, 2–3 orange
peels, and 5–6 juniper berries. Heat
everything up, stirring occasionally and
being careful not to exceed 158°F (70°C).
Pour into a heat-resistant mug and serve.

SUGGESTED USE

A very suitable drink for winter evenings in
the company of friends and family.

IRISH COFFEE

Building method

INGREDIENTS

Irish whiskey 1½ oz (4.5 cl)
hot coffee 3 oz (9 cl)
white or brown sugar 1 tbsp. (20 g)
approx.
cream 1 oz (3 cl)

PREPARATION

Measure 1½ oz (4.5 cl) of Irish whiskey
in a jigger and pour it into a milk jug.
Add 3 oz (9 cl) of hot coffee and 1
tbsp. (20 g) approximately of white or
brown sugar. Heat everything up, stirring
occasionally and being careful not to
exceed 158°F (70°C). Just before serving,
add 1 oz (3 cl) of cream previously
measured in a jigger, using the edge of a
teaspoon so that it remains separate from
the rest.

SUGGESTED USE

An invigorating and energy-boosting cure-all.

ITALIAN COFFEE

Building method

INGREDIENTS

white grappa 1½ oz (4.5 cl)
white or cane sugar 1 tbsp.
(20 g) approx.
coffee 2 oz (6 cl)
cream 2 oz (6 cl)

PREPARATION

Measure 1½ oz (4.5 cl) of white
grappa in a jigger and pour into a milk
jug. Repeat with 2 oz (6 cl) of coffee
and add 1 tbsp. (20 g) approximately
of white or cane sugar. Heat everything
up, stirring occasionally and being
careful not to exceed 158°F (70°).
Pour into a heat-resistant mug and just
before serving, add 2 oz (6 cl) of cream
(previously measured in a jigger) with
the help of a teaspoon so that it remains
separate from the rest.

SUGGESTED USE

A great invigorating drink.

ALCOHOL CONTENT: 14.3
CALORIES: 236

MEXICAN COFFEE

Building method

INGREDIENTS

tequila 1½ oz (4.5 cl)
coffee liqueur ¾ oz (2.5 cl)
hot coffee 3 oz (9 cl)
white or cane sugar 1 tbsp.
(20 g) approx.
cream 2 oz (6 cl)

PREPARATION

Measure 1½ oz (4.5 cl) of tequila in a
jigger and pour into a milk jug. Repeat
with ¾ oz (2.5 cl) of coffee liqueur. Add
3 oz (9 cl) of hot coffee and 1 tbsp.
(20 g) approximately of sugar. Heat
everything up, stirring occasionally and
being careful not to exceed 158°F
(70°). Pour into a heat-resistant mug
and, just before serving, add 2 oz (6
cl) of cream (previously measured in a
jigger), using the edge of a teaspoon
so that it remains separated from the
rest.

SUGGESTED USE

A decidedly flavorful hot drink, it is
perfect for the coldest days of the
year.

ALCOHOL CONTENT: 15.8
CALORIES: 237

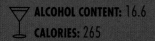

SUPER VIN BRÛLÉ (MULLER WINE)

Building method

INGREDIENTS

red wine 3 oz (9 cl)
brandy or cognac 1½ oz (4.5 cl)
white or cane sugar 1 tbsp. (20 g)
approx.
2 lemon zest
2 orange zest
5 cloves
2 cinnamon sticks

PREPARATION

Measure 3 oz (9 cl) of red wine
in a jigger and pour into a milk
jug. Repeat with 1½ oz (4.5 cl) of
brandy or cognac. Add 1 tbsp. (20 g)
approximately of white or cane sugar,
2 lemon zests, 2 orange zests, 5 cloves,
and 2 cinnamon sticks. Heat everything
up, stirring occasionally and being careful
not to exceed 158°F (70°). Serve in a
heat-resistant mug.

SUGGESTED USE

A great drink to warm you up, it is
recommended for when you have the flu.

In 1946, Frank Capra directed this Christmas fairy tale where the primary mission is to save George Bailey (James Stewart), who is contemplating taking his own life on Christmas Eve. His guardian angel (Henry Travers) orders a Mulled Wine to warm up. Since then in the United States, It's a Wonderful Life and Mulled Wine have become Christmas classics.

IT'S A WONDERFUL LIFE

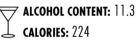
BATIDA DE CAFÉ

Blending method

INGREDIENTS

cachaça 1½ oz (4.5 cl)
coffee liqueur ¾ oz (2.5 cl)
coffee 2 oz (6 cl)
simple syrup 1 oz (3 cl)
white or cane sugar 1 tbsp. (20 g)
approx.

PREPARATION

Measure 1½ oz (4.5 cl) of cachaça in
a jigger and pour in a blender. Repeat
with ¾ oz (2.5 cl) of coffee liqueur and
1 oz (3 cl) of simple syrup. Add 2 oz
(6 cl) of room-temperature coffee, 1 tbsp.
(20 g) approximately of white or cane
sugar, and ½ a tall tumbler of crushed
ice and blend for 15–20 seconds. Pour
everything into the tumbler and serve,
garnished with 2 long straws and a
dusting of ground coffee.

SUGGESTED USE

Ideal to be enjoyed throughout the
evening.

INGREDIENTS

sweet Samos wine 1 oz (3 cl)
coffee liqueur ½ oz (1.5 cl)
amaretto syrup ½ oz (1.5 cl)
coffee 1 oz (3 cl)

PREPARATION

Measure 1 oz (3 cl) of sweet Samos
wine in a jigger and pour into a
shaker. Repeat with 1 oz (3 cl) of
coffee, ½ oz (1.5 cl) of coffee liqueur,
and ½ oz (1.5 cl) of amaretto syrup.
Add a few ice cubes and shake
vigorously for a few seconds. Holding
the ice back with a strainer, strain the
drink into a cocktail gass pre-chilled in
the freezer and serve.

SUGGESTED USE

An excellent digestif, this drink is also
recommended for the hottest days

ESPRESSO MARTINI

Shake and Strain method

INGREDIENTS

dry vodka 1½ oz (4.5 cl)
coffee liqueur ½ oz (1.5 cl)
simple syrup ½ oz (1.5 cl)
coffee 1 oz (3 cl)

PREPARATION

Measure 1½ oz (4.5 cl) of dry
vodka in a jigger and pour into
a shaker. Repeat with 1 oz (3 cl)
of coffee, ½ oz (1.5 cl) of coffee
liqueur, and ½ oz (1.5 cl) of simple
syrup. Add a few ice cubes and shake
vigorously for a few seconds. Holding
the ice back with a strainer, strain the
drink into a cocktail glass pre-chilled
in the freezer and serve.

SUGGESTED USE

Excellent to enjoy after meals or
throughout the evening.

ALCOHOL CONTENT: 10.3
CALORIES: 176

ALPHABETICAL INDEX

BIOGRAPHIES

Gianfranco Di Niso is a professional bartender and winner of national and international competitions. He holds several training courses for freestyle bartenders and baristas. Since 1986, he has worked for many bars in Bergamo, Italy, and its surroundings.

Davide Manzoni graduated from the Università Cattolica of Brescia, Italy, with a degree in Cinema Design and Production. He alternates his love for cinema with his passion for writing. He currently works as a bookseller.

Fabio Petroni studied photography and has collaborated with the most established professionals in this field. His work path has led him to specialize in portraits and still life, and he has shown his intuitive and meticulous style in both these areas. He partners with major advertising agencies, creating several advertising campaigns for prestigious world-known companies, including important Italian brands.

THE TEN BARTENDERS:

Salvatore Bongiovanni has been a professional bartender and sommelier for over thirty years. He is vice chairman of the Classic Cocktail Club and winner of several cocktail contests, both in Italy and abroad. He is owner and bar manager of the Shaker Club Café in Seregno, Brianza, Italy.

Gianfranco Cacciola is a mixologist with twenty years of experience in luxury hospitality, both in Italy and abroad. He has worked at the Four Seasons Hotel Park Lane in London and the Palm Beach in Cannes. He is also the founder of the Barjonio Cocktails project and a trainer in the "Uno chef per Elena e Pietro" school.

Francesco Drago has been a bartender for over ten years. He has received several awards and participated in the 2016 season of the TV show *Mixologist*. He is currently bar manager at Fabrica—Coffee Food Wine, in Trani, Italy.

Silvia Duzioni has been an AIBES (Associazione Italiana Barmen e Sostenitori) barmaid in Italy's Sanremo region since 2008. She has participated in many cocktail competitions and contests and works at the Melograno bar in Urgnano. She is an expert barista and a bar management instructor at the ABF professional training school in Treviglio.

Filippo Fratton has been working in the catering industry for years. His company, NonsoloCaipirinha, offers cocktail bar catering services for events. He has participated in several courses organized by the Organizzazione Nazionale Assaggiatori di Vino, the PBS American Bartending Academy, and Fucina del Bere, as well as in the Lucas Bols Amsterdam 1575 masterclass.

Antonello Gagliardi, after having worked for the best bars and hotels in Bologna, Italy, opened his first bar, Tony's Bar, where he worked for nine years. He also worked as bar manager in other Bologna bars for years. Some years ago, he opened Tu & Yo, a cocktail bar in Bologna.

Vincenzo Giaimo has been a mixology freelance bartender for over twenty years and has been manager and instructor at the AFB, Alta Formazione Barman, of Tuscany. After creating the ERIKA cocktail in Capo d'Orlando, he continued to travel in search of new flavors and arrived in Greece, at the Up Lounge Bar, where he dedicated his signature cocktail list to the flavors of the island of Corfu.

Giulia Gobbi became an instructor at the Federazione Barman Italiana after several courses and professional experiences in catering. She currently works at a well-known restaurant in Rimini, Italy.

Renato Pinfildi is the cofounder of Le Café du Monde, a cocktail and wine bar in Caserta, Italy. He is an AIBES (Associazione Italiana Barmen e Sostenitori) bartender, an AIS (Associazione Italiana Sommelier) sommelier, and a beer sommelier. He is creator and producer of the Wine Cocktail Competition and a member of the Bargiornale 2021 drink team.

Demis Vescovi, worked as a bartender and trainer in important bars in Bergamo and the Costa Smeralda, Italy, after achieving a diploma in hospitality. Later, he had several experiences as an enologist in Franciacorta. He currently works as an enologist in a large winery in Brescia.

The author, Gianfranco Di Niso, dedicates this book to his son,
Alessandro Massimo, who loves to watch his dad work.

ACKNOWLEDGEMENT

Gianfranco Di Niso and Davide Manzoni would like to thank:
White Star Publishers, Valeria Manferto de Fabianis, Giorgio Ferrero, Paola Piacco,
and all the people who contributed to this book.
Fabio Petroni for the amazing photographs.
All the bartenders who enriched this book with their creativity and with ten precious
and original recipes.
Barbara Rota for the constant support that she has always given us.

Gianfranco Di Niso would also like to thank:
MIXER Professional Cocktail Products, which for years has supported the courses he
holds with excellent products.
A special thanks to Luca and Antonella.
All the bartenders and baristas that have supported him over the years.

The authors apologize in advance for any errors or inaccuracies, and they kindly ask
to be quoted as a source when using any material from this book.

EDITORIAL ASSISTANT
Giorgio Ferrero

GRAPHIC DESIGN
Paola Piacco

WS White Star Publishers® is a registered trademark property of White Star s.r.l.

© 2022 White Star s.r.l.
Piazzale Luigi Cadorna, 6
20123 Milan, Italy - www.whitestar.it

Translation: Catherine Bolton, Salvatore Ciolfi, Carlotta Cappato -
Editing: Michele Suchomel-Casey

ISBN 978-88-544-1853-0
1 2 3 4 5 6   26 25 24 23 22

Printed in Serbia